Come to the Table: A Diary of Becoming Catholic

Volume I

By Pamela Henry

Scripture: Holy Bible, Catholic Scripture Study, Revised Standard Version, Saint Benedict Press, Charlotte, NC.

Published by Soul Custody Press

Redlands, California, USA

www.soul-custody.com

Cover image: Leonardo da Vinci's "The Last Supper," public domain usage.

Cover inset photo: Adoration of the Holy Eucharist at The Holy Name of Jesus Catholic Community, 1205 Columbia Street, Redlands, California, August 1, 2025.

Book and cover design by Kamaruddin Ahmad, Bangladesh

ISBN: 978-0-9907848-4-5

Library of Congress Control Number
2026932430

Acknowledgment

To God be the glory!

Dedication

I dedicate this body of work to all people who suffer from disordered eating.

Worldwide starvation occurs in one of every eleven people, according to Action Against Hunger in a United Nations Report, July 30, 2025. Seventy million people suffer from eating disorders, the National Eating Disorders Association finds. And according to researchgate.net, 30 percent of people with eating disorders experienced sexual abuse in childhood.

Untold numbers of people in the world practice gluttony, suffer from active food addictions and diagnosable eating disorders, and worship food as an idol.

May those who come to the table of the Holy Eucharist in the Catholic Church find the missing nutrient for their bodies, in the Body and Blood, Soul and Divinity, of Jesus Christ.

Disclaimer

This diary represents one journey of becoming Catholic as an adult. This is not a book about how to become Catholic, nor does it chronicle the official process of becoming Catholic through the established Order of Christian Initiation for Adults (OCIA, formerly RCIA for "Rite," renamed in November of 2021 by the U.S. Conference of Catholic Bishops).

To learn more about OCIA, contact your local Catholic Church and ask for the formation director, or visit the church's website for information about becoming Catholic.

May the name of the Lord be praised for the book's ministering to its intended readership.

Preface

"And the angel said to me, 'Write this:

Blessed are those who are invited to the marriage supper of the Lamb.'

And he said to me, 'These are the true words of God'."

Revelation 19:9

Nearing Easter of 2025, I asked the Lord in morning quiet time, "Do you want me to take communion?" The response came like the title of a book: "Come to the Table." I wrote down those words. I didn't know it at the time, but I had just received *an invitation to the Lord's Supper.*

The Eucharist, or Holy Communion, is a Sacrament of the Catholic Church that I didn't think applied to me, even though Jesus had long ago said "do this." He said to his disciples: "This is my body, which is for you; do this in remembrance of me." (1 Corinthians 11:24). I was Christian, but not Catholic, and a recovered food addict and alcoholic, free from all forms of alcohol since 1988, and since 2020, free from caffeine, sugar, flour and wheat. Not a drop, bite, taste, or sip, and I don't even eat between four balanced meals. The day's menu is written down in measured amounts to prevent undereating or overeating, photographed, then texted to someone who receives this commitment day after day as if set in stone.

When receiving this invitation, I knew "the table" meant the altar at the nearest Catholic Church, where daily Masses occur. But I was attending a church in Redlands, California, affiliated with the Southern Baptist Convention, where I pretended to take their monthly communion of grape juice and cracker for more than a year. And at the church before that, I pretended to ingest the occasional communion *for a decade.* Both churches served tiny plastic cups and crackers on platters for self-service. I would go through the motions then toss them in the trash on the way out. "Honoring" my abstinence from those substances was lying without me realizing; in pretense, I could hide my food and drink quirks. I don't take a bite or a sip of anything between meals. Even concentrated grape juice, though non-alcoholic, isn't on my food plan, and neither is "the bread."

But all pretense was about to vanish one morning in the light of a Catholic Church. Sitting in the pew at my first Catholic Adoration, where people sit silently in the presence of the consecrated host at the altar up front, a veil in my mind lifted, as if the Lord revealed the prize behind door number one: *I saw that it wasn't "bread and wine."* Speechless, I turned to the person next to me, shouting to them in my mind: "Do I see what *you* see? *That's really Jesus!"*

Once you see, you can't unsee.

Overnight, I went from "that wafer is against my abstinence," to suddenly seeing it as the *Real Presence,* the Body and Blood, Soul and Divinity of Jesus Christ. In the moment of consecration, the earthly element becomes heavenly food for us. *This occurs every day in Catholic churches all over the world.*

This breaking news at age 59 produced my first bonafide *spiritual* craving, way different than wanting coffee or chocolate chip cookies. This is a meal I now must have, the perfect food I've been searching for my entire life in *other* places like Jack in the Box as a kid and Starbucks as an adult. *Why has everyone been keeping this secret from me?* I felt outrage from an unknown source, seeking someone or something to blame so that my own ignorance and lifelong deprivation wouldn't consume me.

This diary is a memoir of becoming Catholic. Officially the journey began with the Order of Christian Initiation of Adults (OCIA) classes at The Holy Name of Jesus Catholic Community in Redlands, California, on August 21, 2025. And the pilgrimage concludes at the Easter Vigil ceremony on April 4, 2026, when new catechumens (unbaptized) and candidates (Christians already baptized) are initiated into the church and get to experience the Holy Eucharist, in First Holy Communion.

I wrote this book convinced that experiencing the Eucharist would feed my soul and explain my lifelong binge eating disorder. It wouldn't be so I could then eat "normally as other people do," but really to provide the missing ingredient my soul had been seeking all my life through excess food. In all the diets from age 12 onward, and now on my current healthy food plan for five years, it never occurred to me that I was missing a heavenly meal on earth every day.

Come to the table. You don't know what you're missing until you respond to the invitation.

Introduction

I really thought it would just be switching churches.

I didn't grow up with religion. My brother and I were baptized as children at the insistence of my Episcopalian grandmother. We didn't even go to church on holidays. Only when I quit drinking at age 22 did I find the God-friendly 12-step programs, which then led me to adopt a non-denominational Christian church.

I've known Stephanie as a 12-step recovery sponsor since 2012, though I kept a blind eye to her Catholicism for at least a decade. I came to accept Christ as an adult in 2013 in response to my eating disorder and wrote my first book about it. I spent a year looking for a church but never even considered the Catholic Church. A new church opened in Redlands in 2014 at the Fox Events Center on Sundays, and I joined my 6-year-old daughter in baptism in the same tank as the first two. My protestant church experience for the last fifteen years has been about attending Sunday church service, leading two people to Christ, inviting people to church, attending Bible studies, bringing my children to church on holidays, and cultivating my own personal relationship with God.

But conversion is defined as: "the process of changing or causing something to change from one form to another." And this is precisely what began in 2025, a total transformation of body, mind, and soul that I was not anticipating. Each step led me closer and closer to the Lord and my experience of Jesus, which is why I decided to keep this diary.

Here's how I came to the table:

After the U.S. presidential election results in 2024, I wrote a personal pledge to not let politics determine my response to life: *I pledge to take full responsibility for my peace of mind, physical safety and health, mental wellbeing, creative endeavors, and primary role as mother. I pledge to keep following Jesus as my sovereign leader and authority, answering to him above all others. I pledge to have a greater positive impact on people in my immediate sphere of influence.*

Little did I know what God was about to do with this pledge of allegiance to Jesus, prompted by a need to not fall apart into the political divide.

Stephanie would occasionally say over the years, "Just go sit in the Catholic Church," and I would do that. I just felt it was her thing, not mine. But she must have picked up on my pledge, because she sent me a book, *This is Our Faith: A Catholic Catechism for Adults* by Michael Pennock. Weekly, I started answering the study questions and sharing them with her. My answers were just perfunctory, but I was warming up to the faith. *I liked the reverence I felt.* Naturally, she said to attend the Easter Vigil ceremony, "the highlight of the year for the Catholic Church," because it's when new people enter the faith. So, I put it on my calendar.

I didn't want to go to the event unfamiliar, so I slipped in the doors of The Holy Name of Jesus trying to be undetected, instead of my other church, on April 6, 2025. The coward in me suddenly emerged, and I hoped no one from church would see me going to Catholic Mass. My secretive, clandestine disposition intrigued me. *Why would I run into them here if they were over there?* What was I hiding? If I had no history with the Catholic Church, why such a strong reaction as if I did have a history? Curiosity set in.

April 6 was already a special day, an anniversary date as the first day I started recovering from binge eating problems in 1991. We remained seated during the distribution of the Holy Eucharist. All I could see was that eating the wafer would be a break in food abstinence for me. I hoped communion wasn't a requirement, because there would be no faking it here. I would attend the vigil to satisfy Stephanie's enthusiasm. But sorry, there would be no getting around that wheat wafer.

From 3,000 miles away, Stephanie knew the time was ripe. She suggested again I *not miss the Easter Vigil service on April 19.* This date also happened to be the release of my newly published book, *Soul Custody: Sparing Children from Divorce.* Attending the Vigil after the online book launch party was a way to give God the glory in a new and bold way, while also appeasing Stephanie.

The church and people looked on fire wearing red like the altar, all aglow with the Holy Spirit. Their holiness and their passion for this event created a curiosity about what I was missing. It felt like someone was getting married and yet there was no couple. I left way too early on that special day, so missed the initiation of new members, completely oblivious to the fact that in a few months, *their* mission was about to become the most important one of my life. When I woke up Easter morning with the scent of ashes from the Catholic Church in my hair, I wanted to go back there, take my three daughters to The Holy Name of Jesus instead of my regular church. But I didn't say a word.

Then, the election of the new Catholic Pope in Rome became a welcome distraction to U.S. politics. Examining the backgrounds of the papal candidates, I marveled at how people come so far in life to reach such high points.

The excitement building in Rome felt like it transcended the political landscape in the United States. The Higher Authority of organized religion seemed an appealing antidote to disorganized politics for the first time in my life.

I stared at the fortune cookie message taped to my laptop computer, feeling the depth of my untapped potential like never before: "You will reach the highest possible point in your business or profession," and realized I'd better *start doing something.* Look how far people go in life! One day, little Robert Francis Prevost is "playing priest" handing out Necco wafers to his friends for communion, and next as an adult, he steps out in front of the world stage as Pope Leo XIV. I wanted someone to look up to, and there he was in all his papal glory, elected May 8. I had my new hero, Pope Leo XIV. I decided to defect.

I chose my 59th birthday on May 18 to give myself the gift of officially attending Catholic Mass, not just trying it, getting my youngest daughter to come with me to mark the occasion. We remained seated in the pew during the communion line. We both grappled with the words to everything. And we talked about her trip to Rome with her school the previous year. "Complicated" was her one-word assessment of the Mass. And then I remembered her telling me when she returned from that trip to Rome: "Mom, I can see why people are Catholic." I retrieved the selfie she sent me of herself in awe during her visit to Vatican City.

Then one day Stephanie sent me Pope Leo's podcast challenging us all to "attend Mass daily for two weeks straight." It felt like perfect timing to respond to such a challenge; it would be a hometown retreat. I chose this daughter's 18th birthday, May 31, because it would honor her into adulthood and usher me into a new faith with fervent prayers for her protection.

My two-week pilgrimage began. I immersed myself in all things Catholic. I read about the first millennial saint that would be canonized and became obsessed over *his obsession* with the Eucharist. I sank further into my book studies to piece together the Catholic crumbs of my childhood, now all seeming like premonitions of "one day" I'd be here. I dared to think I could wear a veil though not Catholic yet and ordered two blue ones from Autom. I'd have to work up the courage to wear a veil. I started tithing to this church and let the other church know I'm converting.

Once I reached two weeks of daily Mass, I didn't want to stop, so I added two more weeks. By then, it was a habit; I didn't want to miss a day. Going on vacation, I found churches in Seattle and Vancouver. The uniformity makes me feel like it's one worldwide church I've joined, not a member of just one parish. I started to feel the power in the words "Jesus loves you" the priest said to me every day, when my turn came in line with the Catholics receiving the Eucharist. The beauty and reverence captivated me. I felt connected to the prayers we said for the world; they felt impactful, all encompassing. And my own prayer intentions felt heard.

I'm becoming Catholic in the Jubilee year of 2025, not even knowing the significance. I'm in the next wave behind the 30 percent increase in numbers of people who became Catholic worldwide in 2024. And I'm among the 160,000 adult Americans projected to join in 2025, approaching levels last seen at the start of this century. Christianity is the largest religion globally, with 2.3 billion followers, and Catholics represent 1.4 billion of them. Read about it at

Catholiconline.news: "Adult Conversions to Catholicism Reach 20-Year High in the United States," Abigail James, August 19, 2025.

May Pope Leo's global prescription for "two weeks of Mass" never run out of refills.

Following my Adoration epiphany where I "saw" the Eucharist for its true essence, I got up the courage to ask the priest after Mass: How do I become Catholic? He smiled like *he'd* won the lottery. But apparently it was I who'd won. Something. Because then he said a blessing over me: "Lord, don't let Satan steal this gift from her." I didn't ask, "What gift?" Nor did I want to wonder how the enemy would steal it. But I suddenly got very protective of whatever he meant. *And if I didn't identify it fast, the enemy might take it without me even knowing!*

Not even a few steps toward my car after his prayer, I was reduced to my childhood fear inherent in saying grandmother's forced bedtime prayer whenever she'd visit: "If I should die before I wake, I pray the Lord my soul to take." One question of the priest and I was already confronting a traumatic interpretation of religion from age five, *that Jesus was going to steal my soul and I had to stay awake to prevent it.* This process was not going to be easy. Could I stomach it? Because now Jesus also wants my body, not just my soul. He wants me in the pew of this church every day to contemplate the heavenly meal until the time comes for me to partake. *And then he wants me to take communion.*

For someone with an eating disorder from childhood into adulthood, it made me wonder how much of my bingeing was about spiritual malnutrition, *not* receiving the Eucharist. I was not fed this truth as a child nor did I seek until now. What if the Eucharist has been the missing ingredient all along – the reason I kept eating more and more? And what if it's the solution to the mystery behind my eating disorder – disordered eating *as a result of not partaking in the Eucharist?*

I wonder why it had to be bread and wine Jesus chose, the two substances I developed addictions to in my life. Maybe I developed addictions because I never nurtured the need for the Body and Blood of Christ. Maybe I developed cravings for sugar and flour that were distortions of the spiritual craving for the Eucharist? I started to see the Eucharist as the mysterious ingredient missing from my current food plan.

This curiosity kept me going through the onslaught of temptations around my eating disorder where I knew that one sip of coffee or one bite of chocolate would send me reeling into the abyss of the void where God feels a million miles away. Because the biggest threat to me in this interim time is the vulnerability around food and drink – the very two ingredients I'm to consume at my First Communion. *Only it's the Body and Blood of Christ.*

I do have fears that when the time comes, ingesting a wheat wafer every day will wake up my dormant flour/wheat sensing brain cells. Currently in remission, I could end up at the donut shop in the afternoon because of ignited cravings. But I already know it's a ploy by the enemy. The enemy doesn't want this daily communion to take place and will fight like hell to prevent me from receiving this heavenly food.

Like I said, I'm 59. Couldn't have someone just said to me sooner, "Do you want to experience true fellowship with Christ? Come to the table, let me tell you about the Eucharist." No. Instead, I collected a lifetime of people who not only hate Christians but bad-mouth Catholics, and I found social acceptance moving in 12-step circles of people *against religion* but "for spirituality." I feel betrayed. All the while for 13 years, Stephanie patiently walked alongside me and my high fortress against Catholicism, dropping clues. She tells me now that one time she asked me if I was interested in Catholicism and I flat out said "No," but I have no memory of even her asking.

Even though the literature in my 12 step fellowships since 1988 says: "Be quick to see where religious people are right," I was quicker to deny the right to choose religion. It was looked down upon as against tradition to even mention religion in 12 step meetings. If you did practice religion, you had to be quiet about it at meetings and certainly couldn't mention Jesus's name in your share without a glare coming your way from someone. I was raised to believe a better approach is to negate your religious views and keep them to yourself, out of discussions altogether. My first 12-step program sponsor in 1991 was Jewish, so I came to know God in the best way possible without Jesus, but it was after meeting Stephanie in 2012 that the Christian life really emerged for me as an adult. To think she waited patiently from 2012 to 2025 for me to peek into her faith, astounds me.

I had *three parents* who could have told me about the Eucharist, especially the cradle Catholic stepmother who as a teen rejected her faith when her parents kicked her out of the house for becoming pregnant. Turns out all my Catholic baggage belonged to *other* people. I have an empty suitcase ready to pack for this new journey ahead! All it contains is a blank book and a pen.

I felt angry at other religions competing for my attention over the years, when this profound truth existed all along. Catholicism was never a competitor among them. The Baptists didn't utter a word about the Eucharist, so I feel lied to by omission. It's a feeling of betrayal. How could the pastors fail to tell me about the greatest miracle of all in the consecrated host? Jesus is in there, in the Catholic Church, the original Christianity. Of course, it's my fault that I didn't come to the table sooner. Perhaps people who feel they have the truth don't feel the need to convince others of it or talk others out of their existing beliefs. I want to view my life through the lens of the Catholic Church. Sign me up.

I just had no idea I was signing up for the magnitude and depth of *conversion,* defined by Merriam-Webster as "an experience associated with the definite and decisive adoption of a religion." That's an understatement. Conversion is nothing short of facing God and turning your insides out, exposing everything to the light. Had I known I was in for the most deeply transformative metamorphosis of my entire body, mind, soul and spirit, well, I would have signed up much earlier in life.

The partial list of issues I had to confront was overwhelming in the three months before I even attended my first OCIA class. I wasn't sure if I was going to get through this maze of my history flashing before my eyes. I was almost frightened away by my own issues before I even attended my first Catholic class:

- Childhood fears of Jesus.
- Traumatic recall of child sexual abuse.
- My divorce from 2008, seeing that through Catholic eyes I'm still considered married.
- Spiritual shame, source unknown.
- Catholic prejudice, source known: my stepmother, religious criticism, doubt and condemnation all courtesy of the enemy, my own misunderstandings and misinterpretations, my own and other's judgments.
- My eating disorder recovery since 1991 and sobriety from alcohol since 1988.
- A real regret failing to nurture my daughters' spirituality growing up.

Like I said, partial list, and that doesn't include the subconscious one. I was going to have to up my game from "just discipleship" and aim for sainthood, but not overnight. These were tall orders. I now questioned whether my entire life I had ever yet experienced anything remotely like commitment to anything other than my own self-interest.

What's in store with this conversion makes my born-again Christian salvation experience in 2013 pale in comparison. But the clues were there during that encounter on the phone with a Christian woman who led me to Christ as an adult in prayer at 1 a.m. on May 15, 2013. Before she said the prayer over me, I told her: "I don't feel God in my body." While the Holy Spirit infiltrated at that moment, like a glorious gold liquid running through my blood, I was still 13 years away from the real thing: First Communion coming April 4, 2026.

Keeping this diary helped me break down the barriers. With each passing entry, the issues were dissolved as ink hit paper. I got good at bringing the next load of personal or spiritual imagery to unpack, especially with Stephanie as my shepherd.

This diary isn't meant to be a record of what OCIA classes involve, but rather what they evoked for me personally along the journey. This is not a book on *how* to become Catholic. It's my conversion experience. I can't wait to see how my life will change when I'm able to have daily communion with the Lord physically in the manner of the Eucharist. I imagine this to be the only Heavenly powered food on earth. It's the experience I was seeking all along in all the other foods, and the source of my true craving that was never satisfied by any other food. All along, I was craving the sweetness only offered by Jesus himself, not a particular food. I thought I had him in spirit but didn't know I could have him in body.

Now I count on attending Mass every morning, and on weekends with the larger morning crowds, I like the afternoon services. I love my ritual. It's the thing I do every day – encounter the Eucharist. And though I can't receive communion yet, there's so much to do to get ready. I filled one journal just in the first three months. That's when I knew a book was in order. The Lord had already given me the title in his invitation, "Come to the Table."

I like to think of my daughter's 18th birthday as an important juncture in my shift to this new phase of my life, typically called the empty nest. There will be no syndrome for me. I'm on a journey of building a nest in the heavenly realm, and while I must wait to gather the heavenly food to go with it, each day is adding a stick to the internal, eternal structure of my soul.

I hope you can find curiosity for yourself in what transpired for me converting to Catholicism. Like Stephanie did for me last year, I would like to invite you to Easter Vigil this year! It's in the evening at your local Catholic Church on the Saturday night before Easter Sunday.

I have an initial assignment for you until then: Attend Mass at your nearest Catholic Church. Get there early and look at the missal in the pew. Find the 1992 song by Dan Schutte called "Table of Plenty" in the index at the back. "Come to the feast of heaven and earth."

Come to the table!

A Diary of Becoming Catholic – Volume I

April 19, 2025

Easter Vigil ceremony

The Holy Name of Jesus

Redlands, California

Outside the church, everyone is standing around a pit of burning ashes. I have no idea what it means, but what's more interesting is how passionate everyone is about festivities. People are buzzing around like someone's getting married; it's such an excitement in the air. I'm just showing up for the ambiance and to get a whiff of what being Catholic might mean. I hope no one notices me.

I'm so excited about my book about sparing children from divorce being published today that I wanted to do something completely out of character for the context of my life. Attending tonight seemed like a nice way to honor and celebrate the accomplishment, by thanking the Lord in a more reverent manner. There's something refreshing about coming here knowing nothing. It's all a blank slate for me.

Or so it seemed. I sat down in the pew, and the ghostly thoughts reintroduced themselves one by one: Catholics were mean, nuns and priests were strict and abusive, Catholic parents kicked my stepmother out of her house at 16 when she became pregnant, and Catholics got films like "Spotlight" made after them. My stepmother made fun of the religion she grew up with and distinguished herself from her sister's devout Catholicism. Catholicism was strict, all about rules, and they were a formal religion. I didn't understand the rosary or communion or confession, but it seemed to me it was all about guilt.

Our family growing up claimed to be Episcopalian but went to church once. My Grandmum insisted we become baptized, my brother and I, when she visited for Christmas of 1975. On that December 28, she accidentally fell outside the church before the baptism. I equated bad things happening around religious things, even though she got up right away. I do recall feeling very holy at age nine during this private family baptism. Grandmum gave me a Book of Common Prayer, containing my record of baptism with a Polaroid photo of us on that day.

Other Catholic snapshots in my mind reappear for context. On November 17 in 1990, I was maid of honor in my sister's Catholic wedding at the chapel at the University of San Diego. The groom was raised Catholic, and the bride was not. It was the most magnificent and long ceremony, followed by a formal waltz they performed at the reception afterward. With so many divorces in our family, I like to proudly claim those two are still married. I got engaged two days after the wedding and think back to how I never asked my brother-in-law for religious marital advice of any sort.

I guess the Catholic history I have is about other people's stories, not mine. Here tonight, it's easy to hide in a huge crowd, just blend in with the stained-glass windows. Suddenly I'm struck with panic. The mounting pressure in my chest chased me right out of the door. I left even before the new members were initiated. *This might be more than just switching churches.*

April 20, 2025

Easter Sunday

I woke up with the scent of the outdoor Easter Vigil ashes on my hair from The Holy Name of Jesus service. My hands still felt aglow just from the warmth of the candlelight and color red all over the altar. Though I fled, an imprint on my soul had been made.

My daughters are comfortable enough with the holidays-only routine of my other church, so I didn't invite them to the Catholic Church today. They expected to attend our regular church. But I felt wistful for yesterday's experience, and curious to return to confront the discomfort I let chase me out the door. *What am I so afraid of?*

May 2, 2025

After having me read John Chapter 6 from the Bible, Stephanie said "just go sit in the chapel during adoration," which starts right after morning Mass. I read that it was a 12-hour adoration, so I decided it would be an all-day retreat spent in the presence of God. I even packed all my meals and water. With a notebook and three working pens, I was ready for some marathon journal writing.

When I got to the church, it was closed. Where is everybody? I was seized with a silence I would soon learn to call Going Mute. A trained journalist, I was *too shy* to call the office and ask, "Where is adoration?" I figured I got the date wrong. So, I went home and unpacked, disheartened, ashamed of my inability to speak up, and with an over-activate case of fear of missing out.

I'll never get back the chance at May 2, 2025 adoration. The loss of my anticipated time with the Lord really felt profound, as if it started to clue me in to the sorrow of living my entire adult life so far not being as close to Jesus as I could be. I care much more about all this than I thought. Not sure which felt worse: that absence, or the exposure of my insecurities, fallibilities and quirks that can't be hidden in a Catholic environment where *everything shows.*

May 5, 2025

I learned why there was no adoration. Our church has a second campus, and that's where the Mass is on Fridays with adoration on first Fridays monthly from 8 a.m. to 8 p.m. Also, adoration is held every Saturday after morning Mass. All I had to do was ask the office that day. Going Mute signaled the giant learning curve ahead.

May 18, 2025

For my 59th birthday, I officially attended Catholic Church today with my daughter, 17, as a gift to myself. I asked her if she would go with me, since it would be my first official regular Sunday Mass attendance. She knew it was a brave stretch for me to leave one church for another because I switched churches before.

Her first exposure to all things Catholic was her trip to Rome with school the year before. I'll never forget the photo she sent me before entering the Sistine Chapel. It's a view from the ground up of her head with the ceiling behind her in a "wow" expression I've never seen. I call this photo "Awe." I'll never forget her first comment about the magnificence of Rome: "I can see why people are Catholic."

Mass today is a symbolic church event for us. When she was six, both of us ran up to be the first ones baptized in the same tank at the new Citizens Church in Redlands. Until now, I didn't know that my first baptism "counted" therefore a second one was unnecessary for me. Now for our new church experience, we sat in the pew while everyone else got into the communion line. We mumbled our ways through words we thought were being repeated during the Mass. It can be jarring to suddenly encounter such ritual and reverence, and neither of us knew what we were doing. But we made a start, and together. I decided it was for me, and she said okay to coming back for Christmas Eve.

June 2, 2025

I've always kept religious and political opinions to myself, having learned at a young age you'll get hurt if you express yourself. But the Catholic Church evokes Truth. So, the first person I must reckon with here is my father. It's like he's standing at the door, even though he died in 2019. I know I confused my Heavenly Father with my earthly father. It's like I'm being asked to separate the two, immediately.

Father's Day is this month, so it's perfect timing for this separation. I'm glad he had me, but he abused my trust, spirit, and body. One time he hit me so hard on the back it knocked the wind out of my 4-year-old body. I had called him stupid for not getting me ice cream while he was at his desk working at home. Ice cream became my favorite binge food, mostly in secret. As an adult when I confronted him, he told me, "I was trying to beat the spirit out of you."

I see why this needs to be brought to the table for inspection. By his abuse, my father had invaded my sacred space, so here he was now where all things sacred converge. During Mass one day, when we prayed for personal intentions, I asked dad to leave this space between me and the Lord. I guess the Lord keeps close to himself things we keep secret. There was no hiding from the Lord how my father's behavior affected my relationship with God. Undetected, it would be enough to keep me away from this church and could have been what sent me running out the door on April 19.

By not claiming this space between me and the Eucharist for me and Jesus alone, I'd be perpetuating my father's invasion of my spiritual privacy, from childhood. I knew physical abuse creates spiritual wounds, but here in the Catholic Church, I saw how it came between me and the Lord. If I'm coming to church here, I can't have my dad in the way. I might even have to forgive him more.

June 6, 2025

First Adoration

Just after returning to the pew after going up in the communion line with my arms crossed across my chest, I watched the consecrated host being put into the monstrance for adoration. Suddenly, a veil lifted in my mind, and *I saw the host as the Body and Blood of Christ right there in front of me.* Not visually, but an inherent knowing, way beyond just believing. Suddenly, the words I'd read made sense from John 6:56: "He who eats my flesh and drinks my blood abides in me, and I in him." *Jesus himself is on this table.*

It had never been so tangible, the Presence of the Lord. Of all the deep meditations I've had where I felt the presence of God, it had never been this real. *That's really Jesus!* All my lifelong feelings of deprivation pooled themselves into receiving this one quenching experience – I could see it was possible to take communion. *It's not just any wafer.* When I take communion for the first time, I know it will fill the void in my soul just waiting for the Real Presence of Jesus.

This felt like an instantaneous discovery, so I turned to the person next to me wanting to confirm, *"Do I see what you see?"* Her eyes were closed as she knelt in prayer, so I couldn't very well confirm with her.

Immediately I felt a target for Satan. Right now, I must ward off everything trying to fill that space I'm carving out for the Eucharist – compulsive job options, objects to buy, finances to fixate on, food I don't need, media overkill, obsessing over my book promotion, daily reasons to miss Mass. If I don't attend daily to get as physically close to the consecrated host as possible, it's like Satan does steal this gift from me. *I still don't know what gift.*

I left the church with the biggest spiritual discovery of my life.

June 11, 2025

What just happened? My life story has shrunk to the size of a pea, and life is coming into sharp focus like a near-death experience. Let's recap:

The Lord called me "to the table." I now know that means the Holy Sacrament of the Eucharist. I started attending daily Mass on May 31 when my daughter turned 18. I have two other daughters, 23 and 27. They grew up in two homes for all the youngest's childhood, a result of shared custody parenting after divorce. Divorced in 2008, I tried to reconcile three times but was told I was too Christian, and that was long before turning Catholic.

I publish my own books as an author and keep diaries. The last book paved the way to this pew.

Converting to Catholicism involves overcoming my stepmother's negative influence since the age of five. She died in 2020.

My Catholic "sponsor" is Stephanie. A sponsor takes an official role as a witness and support person during the OCIA process, helping a new person enter the faith. She started me out with an introductory book on the faith this year.

Tomorrow, I will meet with the formation director at the church.

Everything is about to change...

June 12, 2025

I met with the formation director Rich Mercado at the church this morning after Mass. The enemy attacked me on my way to his office: *"Who do you think you are?"* There are forces that don't want me Catholic, which makes me want to become Catholic even more. What's the enemy so afraid of?

Sitting down at the table, I remembered a dream a few years back. There was an office I was not allowed into at a church, and the priest was inside. Seated at the desk, he saw me at the door and said, *"Who do you think you are coming here?"*

The memory of the dream reminded me again of my father's abuse in his home office, so I was hoping Rich wouldn't notice my flashback as I tried to move forward at the table. *I'm just here to see about becoming Catholic.*

Focusing on facts helped ground me. He said classes would start in August for the Order of Christian Initiation for Adults (OCIA), a spiritual journey for conversion to Catholicism. It involves weekly classes, learning about Scripture, the teachings of the church, the holy sacraments, and involves baptism, confirmation and communion all in one Easter Vigil service on the Saturday before Easter.

We got to the subject of the one marriage of my life, and it turns out if two baptized Christians get married, it's for life. Divorced in 2008, I realized this meant *I was still married in the eyes of the Catholic Church.* How momentarily heartwarming, since I regretted divorcing him. Catholic annulment, however, considers the couple's state of mind at the time of the marriage: Was a true marital sacrament formed? Well, I don't even know what a sacramental marriage is, so perhaps not.

I knew the divorce was wrong; I wrote an entire book about it. But even in that book, I never considered my marriage eligible for annulment. To think I could get right before the sacrament of marriage itself felt like amending my past. I never considered that the union itself might not have been a true marital covenant. He gave me the contact at the church to learn more. So excited about getting right before the Lord on the topic of marriage, I already planned to reach out to her tomorrow.

I learned that in OCIA, I would be called a "candidate" since I'm already a baptized Christian, whereas my unbaptized classmates would be called "catechumens." I put the August date for OCIA classes in my calendar, wondering if I would even stay abstinent from food addiction long enough or would Ben and Jerry's take me out again like it used to do on the way to church Bible studies. But it's a very special day in August that classes are starting – August 21. I once had my longest stretch of food abstinence – 11 years – starting August 21, 1998. These simple coincidences made me feel like a puzzle of a beautiful new landscape coming together.

June 13, 2025

Today I met with a second staff member, about submitting a formal petition for an annulment of my prior marriage to become right before receiving the sacraments of initiation into the Catholic Church. I discovered that a church annulment does not negate the legitimacy of children born within any prior marriage. Only civil law determines legitimacy. In my case, an annulment would not be required before becoming Catholic because I'm not remarried or cohabitating; so, I'm not living in a state of sin.

Motivated, I went home and wrote the petition for annulment according to her instructions. It's for the Catholic Church to determine, but the eye-opening details brought forth as I made my case on paper clued me into two disastrous premarital pitfalls that I had never considered before. Here's one portion of the petition I want to share. It responds to a question about my opinion of why the marriage failed. What came to mind blew me away.

For the petition, I wrote: "The mindset with which I took my wedding vows in 1992 was 'divorce is not an option,' but how I came to that decision was completely faulty. In a spontaneous 'ceremony' during premarital counseling after we got engaged in 1990, the therapist had me walk around my fiancé three times stating 'I divorce you, I divorce you, I divorce you,' to 'get divorce out of my system' ahead of time, since I was so afraid to get married because of my own parents' divorce trauma. What I thought then was a cathartic blessing to purge divorce from my system became a curse. The logic was meant to make me think: 'I can't divorce you when married, because I already did *before* marrying you.' This backfired. This is the reverse psychology I entered the marriage with – that I was already a divorced woman. In essence, I took a vow of divorce before even repeating wedding vows!"

I added to the petition a pre-existing contract with my first boyfriend, the first person I ever had sexual relations with at 15. This never came up in two years of premarital counseling or 16 years of marital counseling, but it did make it into my last book. As teenagers, we decided that if married to other people one day, we could have an affair, and it wouldn't be adultery because we decided it before marriage. I entered my marriage with this hidden contract unchallenged, and he and I ruined my marriage almost 30 years later.

The petition process continues once I become Catholic next spring. I've gone as far as I can at this point. Facing this issue up front unleashed a layer of grief that my one and only marriage wasn't the holy match made in heaven that I once felt it to be; I had entered it with a secret and a curse. Luckily at the same time, the reverence for the idea of the sacrament of marriage and what it really means as a holy covenant filled me with awe and wonder, providing a healing touch to the spot where I was unable to enter a true covenant.

Meanwhile, I'm content being unmarried for life, after all the wrong relationships. I had a five-week fiancé after the divorce, resulting in five years of no dating. Then I had serial fiancés. The last one I married, only to feel such adultery that I sought a civil annulment after five months. Now for four years, being alone has been the purest form of authenticity and peace for me. I finally get to put God first.

June 14, 2025

Saturday Adoration

Eucharistic Adoration is a form of worship in which Catholics spend time in silent prayer and contemplation before the Eucharist in the true presence of Jesus Christ. During Adoration, the Eucharist is typically displayed in a monstrance on the altar, allowing the faithful to come before it on their knees.

My mind felt absorbed into the host. As I sat in the pew, I witnessed an imaginary procession of deceased relatives slowly taking turns in my heart. It's as if they were welcoming me into the faith and smiling about my Catholic journey ahead: My father, mother, stepmother, stepbrother, adopted sister, former marriage counselor, half-sister's mother, and my maternal grandparents. I got the feeling my Catholic-born stepmother winked at me as if she had made peace with her religious past. Maybe I felt their presence because I had put my father's name in the Father's Day novena. But then it got futuristic, as I sensed multiple future grandchildren, all gathering in the realm of my silent heart. I left the church speechless at the enormity of the family reunion.

June 15, 2025

Father's Day

This may be the first time that I really feel the power of prayers said aloud in church, after all these years attending church regularly since 2014. There's something about the collective praying aloud and the kneeling in the pews during Mass that really increases the capacity to believe and receive grace.

The visiting priest said to me in line while others received the Eucharist: "May the Lord bless you and make you an instrument of his love." Later that day I really helped someone struggling with her eating disorder, a cradle Catholic who had drifted.

There are two sides to the binge eating disorder struggle: The people who struggle *not* to indulge in bingeing, and the people who struggle *after* they've already binged. The real help is in the struggle before acting out, the intervention before it happens.

I think the Eucharist is going to show itself as the real solution to my eating disorder. My hope is that it will solve your eating problems, too. I don't know how, I just have a feeling. But you might have to face your father issues first, and any abuse issues, and find out if you, too, have food issues. You also might have to give up binge foods and drinks; imagine the Lord reaching out his hand to take your excesses from you.

Thank God vacation is coming up. We're heading to Vancouver, British Columbia.

July 5, 2025

Vancouver, British Columbia, Canada
Our Lady of the Holy Rosary
646 Richards Street

I desperately had to get here this morning, a spiritual hunger I can't describe. Such a beautiful church! Never be late to Mass; it's sacrilegious. I walked in as the priest lifted the host as it turned into the Body of Christ. *That is not the moment to crash the wedding.* I won't be late to Mass ever again, because of how wrong being late felt.

After Mass, under a banner with the words, "Lord, I trust in you," I lit three candles for my daughters, inserting the cash donations. I trust you, Lord, with my three daughters.

Finding the nearest Catholic Church to attend Mass in any town will be a new adventure now. *Just never be late again.*

What is adoration besides adoring Christ? It is taking in the beauty of silence and proximity of the Presence, seeing my life through this lens. I see myself as a mother, a writer, and an early riser. So much work can be accomplished in pure silence. If you're quiet enough, you can feel God working in the silence within you, changing things, removing things, adding things, even without a pen. It's like God writes onto your heart.

What will I learn in my OCIA classes? How do I tell the Baptist pastors I'm turning Catholic? In the email I drafted to my two former pastors, I wrote that I'm converting because I discovered the truth about the Eucharist and have been called to the Catholic faith where the Eucharist is what I want to experience. Really, I'm coming here because the Lord invited me to the table, and this is where the table is. By adding myself to the Body of Christ, I'll be able to activate the true effectiveness in life I've been waiting for.

A few times, I've wanted to take communion with nobody noticing, maybe go to a church where someone hasn't seen me before, or wait until nobody's looking and sneak a wafer. But when I saw this urge to lie, cheat, steal over a wafer, it felt like trying to have sex before marriage. Then I saw why confession is needed. I'm not even in the classes yet to learn about confession, so let's not.

Confession itself is an interesting prospect. What will I confess? I watched the confession process one Saturday morning. They wait in line in the pews, and each person takes a few minutes. How often do they do this? When do

I get to do this? What will I say? I'm used to Step 10 in 12-step programs, where we promptly admit our wrongs. How is this different?

July 10, 2025

Doubt about taking communion returned as if the veil in my mind had never been lifted that day. I already know I won't be drinking the wine; that's not even an option for me as a recovered alcoholic. At this point in time, I understand the Body and Blood of Christ both to be present in the consecrated host (wafer of bread), thereby making it unnecessary for me to drink the wine. A full communion is made by reception of either species.

How do I know my body won't react the same addictive way even though it's the Body and Blood of Christ? *What if I'm allergic to Jesus?*

When this doubt comes up, I understand why some people deny the Eucharist is really the Body of Christ: It forces us to confront everything between us and the Lord, to come to the table in a holy manner. And everything that's in the way must be inspected. Doubt signals that one of "those" is up again for inspection.

So, no sooner did I get dad out of the way than "family friend abuser," long since dead, shows up between me and the Eucharist. This sacred space was poisoned by sexual abuse at age three. I had no idea I'd have to face this disgust at the prospect of taking the wafer in my mouth. But I'm not alone if 30 percent of people with eating disorders suffered sexual abuse in childhood. The food is a big cover-up operation; if I obsess over the wheat wafer, I don't have to face the abuse. Facing abuse, I'll need to forgive. And I'll need to forgive in order to receive the Eucharist in a worthy manner.

One adoration, I asked the Lord to remove this other man from the sacred space, and he did. This is the work I needed to do while I was married: I never saw my spouse for 16 years as separate from my father's or this other man's abuses. Such abuse results in disgust for the Lord, like a projection damaging the sacred space. I used to project such things onto my poor husband. Now I'm undoing the projections onto the Lord.

And so, before I take communion at the next Easter Vigil for the first time, I have cleared up the *wrong* presence of my father in the spiritual space only meant for the Lord. That's why it was essential to come to the table with this baggage so the Lord can purify the space meant only for me and him. So, when I take communion it's holy, not tainted.

All these years, I believe my pursuit of staunch abstinence was protecting me from the knowledge that dad was hiding in that space meant only for the Lord. What I needed to break free from was dad being in that space, and maybe that's why I broke food abstinence so much over the years before 2020. The same goes for this other intruder on space just meant for me and the Lord. *Good riddance to both their influences.*

The sacrament of the Eucharist is an intentional joining in the Body of Christ, not a break in abstinence. It's almost as though my eating disorder recovery shielded me from the dreadful knowledge of past abuse until I was ready to see it and ask God to remove it. In this manner, through the Eucharist, the Lord will heal that space my father and this other man stole. The Lord will restore the innocent space *before the abuse.* It explains why I felt so apart and alone and explains why I ate food endlessly. I was seeking the Body of Christ, his food, that food.

Not partaking in the Eucharist after discovering what it really is, is a waiting room full of anticipation. I long to feel in communion with the whole Body of Christ, his people. I think it would solve some age-old loneliness of my soul for the past 59 years. I imagine it would make me a more caring and compassionate human being. It will do things for me I haven't experienced yet, because I have never yet become one with Christ in that way.

I go to Mass every day, but I don't feel a part of the Body of Christ yet, not receiving communion. This is not for lack of friendly people or welcoming skills on the part of the church. It's a statement of my separateness without the Eucharist, and hopefully the clearest indicator of why it's so necessary to take it every day, not just Sundays, when I'm able. That's why I come every day even though I haven't partaken yet; I want to get as close as I can to the Eucharist.

July 11, 2025

I feel like I'll connect with people better once I'm receiving communion. It's the way I first felt left out when I *wasn't* eating the treats everybody else was having, sugar items. When I'm able to eat the Heavenly meal with them, this communion will feel like a shared meal.

This limbo state between Baptist and Catholic explains why I've felt ineffective as a worker, a sharer of the gospel, and as a disciple. At my former church only since November 2024, I tried to start a micro-ministry helping couples wait out their urges to divorce, but no one came forward. And when I left the church before that after a decade, I had slowly bowed out of service positions before leaving. I have not even scratched the surface of my potential at age 59.

July 12, 2025

Adoration
Feast your eyes on the Body of Christ.

For the first time, I knelt right in front of the altar on one of the two cushions positioned there for that purpose. I didn't want to go up alone but the woman behind me in the pew wouldn't come with me. It's different than when just sitting in the pew. It's closer to the Consecrated Host. I stared into the monstrance containing the host, and my eyes literally felt fed. Now I know firsthand what it means to "feast your eyes." It was like eating food just looking at it.

And earlier during Mass, did anyone else see Father Thomas's fingertips glowing red as he lifted the cup in this morning's sunlight? If you could feed your eyes, this is how. Surely this could cure blindness even, at least spiritual blindness, and maybe physical, who knows. Do you know that this is the actual Body and Blood of Christ on July 12, 2025, not "back then." You must come see for yourself. *Don't miss a day!*

I see how I can raise my daughters in faith now even though they are all adults; it isn't too late to impart the holiness impacting me. They already benefit from me turning Catholic. Let me count the ways: Mom as part of the Body of Christ means they'll get a fuller version of me, and I will be more connected to them, especially after I'm able to receive communion. Mom's prayers and instincts sharpen with the lens of the Catholic Church on the world and its people. Mom sacramentally sound will be more mentally and emotionally stable. Mom's being permeated with Scripture will offer greater wisdom when they want it from me. Me getting right with Jesus helps me naturally be right with them. They are 18, almost 24, and 27, all unmarried, all in college. I wrote the *Soul Custody* book on sparing children from divorce so that they'd have my lessons-learned blueprint of *what not to do* with the legacy of divorce I handed them. And we experienced familial forgiveness all around through this book, especially from their dad toward me and my eldest daughter toward me.

I can share with them my religious delights and discoveries. They can attend the holidays with me. It will be even more fun when the church is half a mile from my home when they build the new one. There are many, many more people their ages at The Holy Name of Jesus. I see a future when they think of me when they see anything Catholic or anything related to Jesus, just like they do now with anything to do with journal writing, early rising, and earthquakes. They know because of my fascination with earthquakes, I treat them like amusement park rides, no disrespect meant to their worldwide destructiveness or death. Soon they can say, "My Mom's Catholic," and I hope proudly.

July 15, 2025

It's worth noting the mental health miracle that occurred in my life several years ago, because it's an answered prayer of Biblical proportions, now elevated by becoming Catholic. I've been off all psychiatric medications now for three years after being on them for twenty years to treat bipolar disorder, explained in my 2014 published diary. I remained stable even through the death of my mother in 2022. Going off them wasn't intentional; it was a fluke of having Covid in July of 2022. I asked my psychiatrist if he had a medication to treat Covid brain fog, and he felt hopeful a different bipolar medication would work to also address brain fog. So, I took the new one as I weaned off the old one. The new one backfired, so when I stopped taking it before reintroducing the old one again, it was like a window of wellness opened. He watched me for nine months, anticipating something would go wrong, but I only got better than ever so left his care altogether.

I knew I had to pull out all the stops if I was going to remain off medication, so I asked in deep prayer for a miracle on my mind in the same vein as the healing stories of the Bible. If it worked for them, it could work for me. It also helped by being off all sugar, flour, wheat, caffeine and excess food, exercising daily, not practicing any addictions, and remaining chaste from relationships. I also adjusted my life to suit the pace, making things simpler on to-do lists, sleeping well, praying more, working less, and everything seemed to embrace a life without medication. For someone diagnosed with bipolar disorder, which usually doesn't just go away, this was indeed a medical miracle. *It was a modern-day Biblical miracle.* Becoming Catholic is awakening brain cells I never knew existed. My dream life even returned.

July 16, 2025

St. Elizabeth of Hungary Catholic Church
Desert Hot Springs, California

I always visit the desert in the dead heat of summer, loving the intensity and spirituality of it. Today the priest at this desert church physically made the sign of the cross on my forehead. It felt like a healing balm for my mind. Now he's putting the host in the monstrance. It really feeds the soul to sit in church and hear the elderly ladies say the rosary with such devotion and conviction and feast my eyes on the host. One day I will be one of those elderly ladies.

Speaking of our elders, here at this church I ran into Virginia, the mother of my oldest adult friend Molly who never told me her mother was Catholic, or if she did tell me, I tuned it out. I knew this was her hometown, but not her church. We jumped for joy seeing each other, as she had no idea I was becoming Catholic, and Molly doesn't know yet. Through Virginia, I invited them both to the Easter Vigil.

I thought about how to tell Molly this spiritual news of mine, and it came to me:

If you were personally invited to the Eucharist by the Lord, would you turn it down?

Oh, to be a saint! Get ready to laugh, because aside from Mother Teresa and Saint Francis of Assisi, I *didn't know they were real people in history.* And I didn't know there were so many saints. I thought saints and angels were fictional. But these saints as ordinary people are role models who are declared saints only by the Catholic Church. Catholicism has brought the saints down to earth for me, and the angels alight in heaven.

Knowing they were real people made me want to become a saint, too, but it felt arrogant, so I didn't tell anybody of my heart's new aspirations. What type of saint would I want to be? First, my name means "all honey" in Greek. *I'm so sweet I don't need sugar.* So, I'd love to be the patron saint of helping people become abstinent with their foods, from sugar, flour, wheat, caffeine and excess. I could help a lot more people if I thought of myself as a saint able to help people achieve abstinence.

The other qualification is I could be a patron saint of saving marriages, because my divorce wound is a sacred wound that God has turned into glue for other couples. At least that's how it felt to write my last book. Not that anyone has lined up to buy them. Lord, show me my sainthood! Is everyone capable of being a saint? Is sainthood our true potential? Is everyone meant to become one? Stephanie said I must pursue sainthood, but with a small "s." It's news to me that Catholics aspire to sainthood.

I read about holy orders, and it made me think of my callings. I'm called to help married parents who think of divorcing, stay married; bring them back from the brink. Is the petitioner like me, wanting out just to escape issues arising in response to past trauma? Escapist divorces, I call them. I'm called to help people with eating disorders. And I'm called to the table to become Catholic. As I writer, I felt called to write this book to draw others to the table.

I want to get a veil to wear to Mass but I feel embarrassed wearing one not being Catholic yet. Can I? I'll ask Stephanie. I don't want black (funerals) or white (shouldn't it be off-white at my age?). I saw a dark blue one the color of the forelight sky. That's the one!

July 17, 2025

AI spells it out when asked, "How to aspire to sainthood." It's much easier than I thought. But it says not to make it a personal goal. But wouldn't it be the highest aspiration a human could aim for? Certainly, we can't become angels. Aren't we supposed to be like Jesus, isn't that the whole point of "Follow me"? Here's how AI answered:

"Becoming a saint is a complex and rigorous process within the Catholic Church, requiring a deep commitment to faith, service and spiritual growth. Here's a general overview:

Spiritual growth:

1. Develop a strong faith. Cultivate a deep relationship with God through prayer, devotion and reflection.

2. Live a virtuous life: Strive to embody virtues like compassion, humility and kindness in your life.

3. Serve others: Engage in acts of charity, volunteer work, and service to others.

Catholic Church requirements:

1. Live a life of heroic virtue. Demonstrate extraordinary devotion, charity and selflessness.
2. Perform miracles. In some cases, miracles attributed to the individual's intercession may be required for sainthood.
3. Undergo canonization process: The individual must be declared "venerable" by the Pope, followed by beatification and eventually canonization.

Important notes:

Sainthood is not a personal goal. The focus should be on serving God and others, rather than seeking sainthood. The process is lengthy. Canonization can take many years, even centuries. Only the Catholic Church can declare someone a saint. The process is specific to the Catholic Church and its traditions. Ultimately, the path to sainthood requires a profound commitment to faith, service, and spiritual growth. If you're interested in learning more, consider consulting with a spiritual advisor or exploring Catholic Church resources." (End AI lesson).

This lesson helps me see that I'm at the *very immature level of seeking sainthood as a personal goal and* have much work to do. "We are not saints!" declares the basic text of Alcoholics Anonymous. That's why I didn't think I could be in the league of saints, and it never occurred to me to aspire to them, since I thought all but two were imaginary anyway.

But I was wrong to keep a lid on my holy potential. Josette, the first Redlands church member to shepherd me into the flock, brought this concept down to earth for me in her group emails addressing us as "Dear saints."

She expects us to unleash that potential! I'm coming from having only used that word as a joke about someone who thinks too highly of themselves, and now I'm throwing it around as household word; this is just one way Catholicism brings heaven down to earth.

Back to that fortune cookie message I taped to my computer screen in 2024: "You will reach the highest possible point in your business or profession." Secretly I hoped it meant my last book would be a best-seller to prevent divorces. But what if it means I take the high road and aim for serving God and see where it lands me? In this morning's quiet time, I tried on the ambition for size, and the shoe didn't fit. For months, I couldn't connect with any couples through my other church when I wanted to intercede before a spouse would file for divorce. But what if God makes a way for me to meet with them, pray with them, and bless them, through me being Catholic now? The veil would be lifted on the wanna-be petitioner to see their marriage in a new light. In one meeting, by inviting the Holy Spirit in, Jesus would heal the marriage.

This divorce wound in me became a sacred one for me, meaning I can see its potential for my ability to help parents because of my own healing. And I see the saints have more than one specialty they can be called upon for. There's no reason I can't help people with all addictions, especially eating, and saving marriages, too. But I have an embarrassing amount of character development that must happen before I'd ever actually *live up to it.* I can't even write without pride yet, surely you can tell.

July 18, 2025

His name was Father Arinze Ezeoke! He is the priest at The Holy Name of Jesus who prayed over me when I asked, "How do I become Catholic?" I hadn't seen him in church since, but that's because he relocated. That day he showed me a newsletter with the Catholic formation director Rich Mercado's email address on it. Then he said a prayer over me, and the distinct words I recall were: "Lord, don't let Satan steal this gift from her." My mind raced: Is the gift the desire to become Catholic, is the gift the invitation to come to the table, or is the gift the calling to this Catholic Church? When and how was the gift given? What exactly is the gift? When he said it, I didn't know what gift he meant that the enemy would try to steal. I felt invincible until now, but what should I be on the lookout for? If you don't know what could be stolen, you don't know how to guard it!

I ordered a blue veil that came in a two-pack from a website called Autom. It's my favorite color, forelight blue, the dark blue before dawn, the time of day I wake up during what's known as the Fourth Watch. I'm too shy to wear it yet. That's another snare the devil uses – potential embarrassment. Like one day I'd like to be someone who gets to read Scripture from the lectern at church, but the enemy reminds me I'll mispronounce Biblical names.

For now, I'm a leaf in the wind, either ready to be consumed by a fire or crumpled into pieces from dryness. This is how my soul feels, apart from the tree trunk or the vine that I'm waiting to connect with. *Why do I have to wait until April?* I already believe in the Eucharist. I must be very careful in this dry spell I'm in. I could get greedy even over the Eucharist, even envious of those who get to do it. I have felt fully my apartness from the Body of Christ like never before, and it feels a bit like being an empty shell. I wonder if this feeling is what some people just call loneliness, but it's really longing due to the decades of separation I'm finally noticing.

The reason I feel this space so intently is I'm not filling it anymore with certain foods and drinks, or excess of any kind. I eat four meals a day and only drink water. I'm a complete empty vessel. In this waiting period, I can learn about boundaries, protection, snares, and saying no, prayer, patience, and respect. Surely God is preparing me for something. For now, I feel erased. Eating more food won't make me visible like I once thought – it would further erase me from this process of becoming Catholic. *Don't reach for that cup of coffee or cookie. That alone can steal my gift, like Eve's apple bite.*

July 19, 2025

Indulge me for a moment in sainthood formation, third person. I'm imagining that Saint Pamela was born at 4:41 p.m. on May 18, 1966, at Presbyterian Medical Center in San Francisco, California. The family lived at 3478 Clay Street. She kept journals at a young age. *But what does she do that's saint-like?* My motive is to be of greatest impact for the glory of God.

I think sainthood is in my own home with my influence on three daughters and helping them with their children one day. I really am not sure of any bigger picture than this, especially because I'm so bad at publicity, promotion, and social media. Any loftier thinking beyond motherhood feels inflated and out-of-bound. So, I guess I just want to be a saint to them. That's good enough for me.

Becoming Catholic is a journey to the original Christianity with the Eucharist. This is the spiritual food I've been seeking all my life by overeating. I'm hungry, but it's for the Body of Christ. I see my entire binge eating disorder now as a manifestation of not having the Eucharist.

It's eating disorder meets the Eucharist. Do I try to be among the people with celiac's disease and ask for a low-gluten alternative, or do I trust the transubstantiation process that the minimal wheat composition won't trigger my addict brain cells now dormant for five years? Maybe my soul will be fed, but my body will carry me to Yum Yum donuts at 3 o'clock that day, having been triggered by a wheat wafer from morning Mass. *Those addict cells sleep rather than expire.* And yet I have this hope that my body won't react the same way to the Body of Christ as it does, say, a Triscuit, which really means the whole box. I also don't want to hold up the communion line while they fish for the alternative wafer meant for "that girl."

I don't even start my OCIA classes until August 21, but I go to Mass daily with some exceptions having to do with my children. Each time I go up front in the communion line, I cross my arms over my heart and the priest says, "Jesus loves you." I love hearing this but feel left out of the big feast. Eucharist is a daily feast, the daily experience of being with the Lord! Why would you want to miss a day? The Eucharist. Greek word, "eucharistia," meaning thanksgiving. Expressing gratitude for Jesus's sacrifice at the cross. In the "Our Father" I've prayed my entire life, it says, "Give us this day our *daily* bread." Never once have I experienced it. Yet.

Every day with the Eucharist, *we don't have to wait for his second coming!* Each Mass, he comes right down before our very eyes in transubstantiation, a cool word meaning "the change of the whole substance of bread into the substance of the Body of Christ, and the wine into the Blood of Christ." It's like he walks right in the front door of every Catholic Church in the world when his spirit descends like the dewfall upon elements on the altar. And we all share in his presence in communion.

The Eucharist is the best-kept secret on earth.

July 21, 2025

Now I'm really thinking the reason my eating was disordered my entire life until the last five years, is that I was missing the Eucharist, not receiving the Body of Christ. I haven't had it yet, but I know what's waiting for me. Because I will be at one with the Body of Christ, not apart from it. Bingeing on bread was really a symbolic longing for Jesus.

In binge mode, I was really trying to hit that spot inside only meant for the Eucharist, but eating could never touch it. Because no matter what food I chose or how much, it would never satisfy. Imagine the missing puzzle piece being put in place, only I am the puzzle piece being put into the Body of Christ. Because right now the Body of Christ exists without me, but I as a puzzle piece of a person, will be added to it. That's when I'll be able to make real connections with people and have a greater impact in his name. Because I will be moving within the Body of Christ for once. The distinction I'm trying to make is important, because in the two decades I studied Unity School of Christianity principles out of Unity Village, Missouri, I believed Christ was already within me. *But I was not in him.* There's a difference. The spirit of Christ may have been in me since baptism, but his actual body, never yet.

July 22, 2025

Formal religion is new to me. I joined churches before but never intentionally decided upon a religion. I didn't even really understand my non-denominational status for years; to me that just meant neutrality and that I didn't commit to any denomination. I didn't even know when I joined Pathway in Redlands what it meant being part of the Southern Baptist Conference of churches. I didn't even know what set Baptists apart from Catholics. I paid no attention to the difference between Catholics and Protestants. I tuned out any religious disagreements ever brewing around me.

I love the reverence in the formality and structure of Catholicism. They really know how to practice silence. Just come witness the respectful silence during Adoration, how people honor and experience the Presence of Jesus through the Eucharist. The words said during Mass are starting to make sense to me. The routine has already built a new foundation to stand upon in my life.

As soon as I decided *Come to the Table* would be a book about becoming Catholic, the enemy tried to lure my pen away. It feels like the enemy rejoices when someone loses faith, skips Mass, works on a Sunday, or in the case of writing a book, chooses *any* other topic but becoming Catholic. Taking the bait, I'd find yet another distraction, such as a relationship to fixate on, a job I can't refuse, preoccupation with possessions, or once again, binge foods. Whether it's shopping for a used car, the cat dying, and anything going on with other people in my life, all of it can throw the focus of Jesus in a split second. Though sobriety from alcohol always feels intact, there's a risk I could lose my food abstinence between now and April 4, 2026, or even before OCIA starts next month. Food is so easy to lose abstinence over.

A feeling of futility comes over me thinking of putting this book together. I'm not even Catholic writing a book on becoming Catholic. I feel unworthy. But so did the centurion in the Bible when he came to Jesus to heal his servant, and we say it during Mass every single day: "Lord, I am not worthy that you should enter under my roof, but only say the word and my soul shall be healed." I feel like no matter how unworthy I feel, the Eucharist is the last word on my eating disorder.

It's clear that the enemy wants to steal my pen and loves it when my ink runs out. This is why I send a candle emoji on the phone to Stephanie to keep accountable for my daily writing commitment, except on Sundays. Thy will be done, Lord, on all my employment and in all my comings and goings. Satan's tricks are so repetitive, but they increase in severity when the stronghold is up against the Lord's magnificence at key junctures. And becoming Catholic is my biggest one yet.

It never occurred to me until now that by not doing communion, I wasn't doing what Jesus was asking of me. I thought it was just something symbolic other people did. Why did I consider myself an exception? I'm late to the feast, making up for lost time.

July 23, 2025

I do fear intimacy with God and being in communion with the body of Christ. My eating allowed me to have a buffer and a barrier, where I didn't feel so visible, even to God. Now I will be transparent before God and people and have no place to hide, not even in "my coffee" since I don't drink it. The irony is that I must go to God with my fear of him and let him work it out of me. And I must go to people to overcome my fear of people. It's a Catch 22 on both.

Lord, I fear becoming more intimate with you in communion. I already feel the awesome power of your love. I feel that you'll reveal big things in me or about me or for me to do that I'll feel inadequate to perform.

Maybe this is just typical performance anxiety of the sexually abused. Unwanted sexual advances cause a person to not know what to do. I had that feeling of knowing something was wrong but being powerless to stop it. Why I've confused it with becoming closer to God, I don't know. I think trust in a parent is a child's trust in God, and this uneasiness with my father breaking trust in my childhood made me feel the same way about my Heavenly Father, that he would ask too much of me and I would prove inadequate to the task.

August 13th starts my 33-day self-imposed pilgrimage in the "33 Days to Eucharistic Glory" book by Matthew Kelly that Stephanie sent me. There are certain dates to start and end and this one puts me at ending on the day of the Exaltation of the Holy Cross for Eucharistic consecration.

I must have a long way to go claiming my faith because it all sounded so silly to me when I told my oldest daughter, 27, about becoming Catholic. *She laughed.* I didn't ask why she thought it was funny, and I'm certain she wasn't mocking me. I told her how after attending Mass for two weeks straight I didn't want to stop, having seen that communion is really with the Body of Christ, not just his spirit. But it all landed so wrong, like I don't know how to talk about it yet. It surprised her because it sounded so randomly occurring, like who wakes up and says, "I think I'll become Catholic today." *But belief in the Eucharist did happen to me in an instant that one day.* I invited her to church. She said she tried the Catholic Church once in college with a friend, but it wasn't for her; I didn't know that.

I just wish I could have announced my conversion in a more profound or meaningful way. I'm surprised –no, more like mortified – that I kept it quiet for *two months* like some family secret. Now that I've addressed divorce regret, I'm looking at spiritual neglect of them. Why didn't I formally help nurture their spiritual lives? How would I ever make up for it now?

Talking to my daughters about Catholicism, what a challenge. I have a new opportunity almost every day when any of them asks me, "How was Mass?" And I feel victorious if I come up with anything beyond, "Fine." I didn't raise them in faith, so it's a first. My mother and I never discussed religion or God my entire life, how sad.

My youngest knows the most from me so far about becoming Catholic. I did explain that I wanted us all to attend the Christmas Eve service this year at the new church and already invited them to the Easter Vigil initiation ceremony next spring. I'll have to find a voice of faith as a mother. It isn't too late for that, even though they are adults already. I missed my chance of raising them in faith. I just know if my grandmother hadn't insisted, I wouldn't have been baptized as a child. I am more at risk for going mute than being overbearing. I'm not sure which is worse; probably silence.

In the process of becoming Catholic, I face my fears at every turn now. The enemy whispers, "You're going to trigger food cravings if you eat the wafer." Saint Michael protects us from the snares of the devil. The devil works overtime when it comes to me and food, but I *never* give in no matter how much he tries to tempt me like Eve.

July 24, 2025

The peacock dream last night: This must be my deadly pride in all its full color glory. Giant bird, the size of a building! Approaching me then spreading its wings. In the dream, I was taking a video of the peacock. Online it says when a peacock appears in a dream, it shows you that you are very confident in yourself. "It could also portend selfishness and arrogance. Don't forget you need help from other people." So while the peacock represents love, kindness, wealth, change, prosperity, divine protection and good luck, in my case he's probably here to warn me about the reduction of ego.

It's humbling to be lumped in with an institution under such attack and simultaneously blamed for doing all the attacking on others. I didn't think I'd have to defend myself on social or political issues, stances the Catholic Church takes. Can't I just become Catholic to know and love and serve God more? Do I have to take stands on moral and social issues? Is my joining the church an unspoken agreement for everything the Catholic Church stands for?

Today I gave the Jesus Hands Thrift Store in town the wedding dress that endured two failed engagements. It was once $1,600 and meant for my canceled wedding on May 4, 2018, at the Fox Events Center in Redlands. But it's also the dress I wore in an epic dream that is making sense to me only now. During that engagement failing, I had a dream I was at the church service held on Sundays at the Fox Event Center, and all the church members were there. Suddenly, I started spinning like a tornado spiraling upward in my wedding dress. There was no groom in sight, but everyone was in awe as I spun and rose. I woke up completely transformed by the dream. At the time, I didn't even know what the concept of being the bride of Christ meant. And that the church itself *is the bride of Christ! He is the bridegroom.* Now I wish I had saved the dress from the dream. But I wonder who ended up buying it and for what bargain price? I asked the ladies at the store to pray over it before selling to refresh its twice-failed-engagement vibes. The dream now feels like it foreshadowed what occurs April 4, 2026. *It's the marriage supper of the lamb.*

I looked it up: "Christ is the Head of this Body" (CCC 792) and The Church is the Bride of Christ (CCC 796). *People are the church.*

Formal religion is new to me. I joined churches before but never intentionally decided upon a religion. I didn't even really understand my non-denominational status for years; to me that just meant neutrality and that I didn't commit to any denomination. I didn't even know when I joined Pathway in Redlands what it meant being part of the Southern Baptist Conference of churches. I didn't even know what set Baptists apart from Catholics. I paid no attention to the difference between Catholics and Protestants. I tuned out any religious disagreements ever brewing around me.

I love the reverence in the formality and structure of Catholicism. They really know how to practice silence and keep the focus on Jesus. Just come witness the respectful silence during Adoration, how people honor and experience the Presence of Jesus through the Eucharist. The words said during Mass are starting to make sense to me. The routine has already built a new foundation to stand upon in my life.

As soon as I decided *Come to the Table* would be a book about becoming Catholic, the enemy tried to lure my pen away. It feels like the enemy rejoices when someone loses faith, skips Mass, works on a Sunday, or in the case of writing a book, chooses *any* topic over becoming

Catholic. Taking the bait, I'd find yet another distraction, such as a relationship to fixate on, a job I can't refuse, preoccupation with possessions, or once again, binge foods. Whether it's shopping for a used car, the cat dying, and anything going on with other people in my life, all of it can throw the focus of Jesus in a split second. Though sobriety from alcohol always feels intact, there's a risk I could lose my food abstinence between now and April 4, 2026, or even before OCIA starts next month. Food is so easy to lose abstinence over.

July 25, 2025

I wore my blue veil today for the first time! It was natural, not a big deal at all. It felt protective. What does it mean to wear it? Aside from the product description: blue lace traditional chapel veil, two-pack for $16.39 plus $10.99 shipping. My eldest daughter tried it on; she looked so holy! We couldn't figure out the proper angle, but then I did — it goes flat across the back and the pointy angles hang down on each side in front.

A lot of becoming Catholic is looking stuff up online when too shy to ask anyone. I found out: It's called a mantilla. The purpose is to remind us of the spousal relationship between Christ and the church. It's a reminder of the sanctity and dignity of women. The veil symbolizes being worthy of protection, holiness, reverence, and surrender to God's will. It's a visible act of modesty and humility, a visual statement and public proclamation before the Lord that He is the Lord and that we love him and are ready to obey him. I felt quieter wearing it, as well as shielded from other people's opinions, especially about my stringy hair now covered up. So, it enables me to think of myself *less*. With all the stuff going on in the world, what better time to pause and consider *the veil.*

In my faith work with Stephanie, I learned a new word today, considered a sin: Apostasy. It's rejection and denial of faith. Ignorance doesn't count; it has to be intentional. But knowing what I know about the Eucharist now, it would be akin to apostasy for me to not receive the Eucharist next spring. It feels like apostasy already just to skip Mass for even a day, even for "valid reasons." It's not about getting into trouble with the Catholic Church or God being mad at me. It's something called *conviction,* which I now have, and *devotion,* both needing their daily bread.

July 26, 2025

Adoration begins. I write. Today I'm aware of how close I got to the consecrated host when the priest said, "God bless you." I felt the bowl in front of my face, and I could practically taste it just by looking. This is what I have craved for 59 years, to be in communion with the Lord. I'm certain this lack of union is why I've felt untethered mentally, physically and spiritually, emotionally, missing this element, and one bite away would connect me to the Body of Christ per his original instruction.

In my first 12-step food program in 1990, we learned to abstain "from that first compulsive bite" like an alcoholic does the first sip, and so any bit of sugar, flour or excess would be a break in abstinence, a kind of fall from grace similar to Eve in the Garden of Eden. That his body is now one bite away is what helps me receive grace now, so the irony of the contradiction is not lost on me. This is not a first bite of addictive food, but the one bite that was missing from every food plan since I began recovering in 1990. From every food plan was missing the one bite of the body of Christ that would bring me in communion with the Lord. *So acute is the separateness I now feel!*

I must write about this angst in greater detail to see if you want to come to the table with me. Here are some questions to ponder:

- Do you feel an emptiness and a craving in the deepest part of your soul that you have tried to fill with cookies, ice cream and coffee, only to wonder why the craving just increases?
- When you look at people, do you just see other moving bodies in front of you, scanned by your own split-second mental assessments?
- Do you not feel the presence of these people but just their physical appearance before you?
- Do you feel a connection to a stranger or are you glad to avoid them, glad you don't see anyone you know?
- What is the source of your loneliness?

Today mine is recognizing 59 years apart from the host and having to wait until spring before I be in communion with the body of Christ. I have not understood the separation I feel from people all my life, until now. I've always been around so many people but separate from them at the same time! I didn't know that there was another way to be connected to Jesus to be connected better to people in the world. It explains why I've been so limited in my ability to love and create enduring partnerships. Even in my marriage from 1992 to 2008, I missed the sacramental part of it altogether. He missed it too, and therefore our children missed seeing it. For that I feel very sorrowful — that we failed our children spiritually by not showing them what marriage means to God.

Today, these three little girls have grown up. They are not in my mother-hen care anymore day to day for every next move. They even want to make their own food. I don't shepherd them through the day, take them to and from places, tuck them into bed, or read them stories at night. Even if they have children one day, this will be their role with them, not mine, but at least I'll get to be a Catholic grandma.

Sad that at 59, if I'm a leaf in the wind, seeing my daughters as little dandelions floating on the winds of the world, tethered to what, I don't know. What do they feel tethered to? What is their anchor? What grounds them? Certainly not mom's faith. And even my faith...how much can it do for them? What can I give my girls now, Lord? It's not like I have any marital relationship credibility to offer them hope for their futures; divorce ruins that. It's not like they'll see me become Catholic and suddenly decide it's for them, too.

Lord, how will I help my girls with faith if I do have any in-roads or input? Will you make it clear? I missed the first round. I'm so sorry, Lord, that in my mothering of them, I neglected to spiritually nourish my children. I have been spiritually starved just by being ignorant of the host, by the absence of the Body of Christ. How am I going to last these next months? Maybe OCIA classes starting will be enough; I'll feel collected in a basket with all the other floating leaves. *It's less than one month away!*

Lord, thank you for all you have given me in my life, the financial security as a single mom to take care of my three girls and write, without needing a life partner, a safe home, good health and evolving character, joy and peace in the turbulent modern times. In church today, the priest asked, "What is the Lord asking of you?" I'm not sure what you are asking Lord beyond come to the table and keep writing, but I'll try to live each day as if I'm ready.

July 28, 2025

Doubt sounds like this: What if my own faith journey begins and ends with me, and isn't about imparting anything at all to anyone else? That was the enemy using discouragement after a fallen-away Catholic told me: "No one cares about your own personal journey; what would it mean to them?" My feelings were hurt. But then I got to thinking, what if she's right? What does my diary mean to you if it's all about me? Online, I confirmed it: A Catholic publisher is not taking submissions of personal conversion stories. Are we a dime a dozen and she's right?

Anyway, I turned it into an opportunity to formulate faith. What if my book is meant to draw Catholics back to their own faith? What if my book sends people with eating disorders to the Eucharist with the same hope I have? She's disenchanted; maybe I could test out my manuscript on her. There's hope, because she agreed to review it for me.

I'll let you know how that goes. Meanwhile, don't let other people's Catholic experiences, including the abandonment of them, taint your own. I haven't even begun to tap my potential because I'm not even one with the body of Christ yet sacramentally. Thank God I didn't give up on life in the first book I wrote, *The Resting Place, A Graveside Diary*, before knowing there was so much more ahead.

We'll see. I only have the limited vision of seeing all this from *outside* the body of Christ, not *in it* yet. I'm only outside the Eucharist looking in, not yet fortified by its transformative power. Lord, I trust this conversion experience isn't just for me but for anyone else looking on in the future, whether reading this or witnessing me, that they be brought home to you as I was a prodigal daughter without even knowing I was away from home. Be it that others benefit. Amen!

July 31, 2025

Today on my middle daughter's 24th birthday, I know how much you love me Lord because I get to be the mother of these three young ladies, and so the love I have for them, if it's anything like the love you have for me, we're good. I went into labor with this one while in a 12-step meeting at the St. Francis of Assisi Catholic Church in La Quinta, out in the California desert near Palm Springs. She was baptized by a Catholic priest in Montana at a year old.

My prior Catholic connections are returning like puzzle pieces. They're making me strong in body, mind and soul and spirit to be a conduit to a spiritual anchor for my daughters. Just my presence with them is all that's required, because each and every word from me will be filtered by the heavenly host, O Lord, even before I partake!

Mass is now my favorite part of the day, and Eucharistic Adoration my favorite Catholic experience. I say the Spiritual Communion Prayer meant for those of us who can't partake yet in communion. I'll have to learn to be more outspoken, rather than wimpy or silently condoning. I learn from my adult children the most these days.

Here's a personal essay this middle daughter wrote that inspired me:

"This time is calling me towards more activism, more community building, more local connection and positive relationships with others around me. I want to connect with my local community because at this point I feel like it's all I can do because making a big change in the world right now feels impossible. Maybe our small strides can be enough to make an impact. It sure does feel really hard and impossible right now and it feels like things in the country and world as a whole are scary and taking a bad direction. But I think right now we need to rely on each other and find comfort in our local communities. We can grieve together and also advocate together. I'm in my 20s right now and I hope that by the time I'm ready to start a family that I can have more confidence in the leaders in our country and know that I'm in a safe place with the same rights as everyone in this country. We should all be there for each other in these hard times."

As an exclamation to her point, there was a 4.5 earthquake today in nearby Fontana. I was outside and the ground shook, everything outside shook, and I felt it under my feet in Redlands. It seemed to say: "Wake up! You've been spiritually asleep and it's time to wake up. People need help. Get out there and help them."

It would be Biblically correct, and certainly overdue in Southern California, to have an earthquake right about now. Are you ready? You may know how to love your neighbor, but do you know how to save them?

August 1, 2025

First Friday Adoration

Lord, I bring to you my lifelong wounds, no match for yours.

The healing I still need confronts me at the Eucharist. I think of Jesus's wounds, and how all my bodily wounds will be healed the moment I receive the Body of Christ – because his wounds will cover mine. *Because he died for these very wounds, and the Eucharist is meant to heal them. You can only go so far without Christ.* There are voids within, spaces waiting to be filled by the Holy Spirit, but they have to stay empty for now. Don't fill them with things or jobs or distractions or spending or numbers of people I sponsor in 12-step programs for food and drink. Help one person at time.

Lord, it's the unsaid and the undone I'm worried about. Are there any connections I'm not making that I should be making, and if so, can you make them louder?

Three more weeks until OCIA classes start. I walked this morning in beautiful sunlight. All my ages in history seemed to merge. All days before now seemed to merge into today, and all days to come also merged into today. There is no place I would rather be than in church right now on a summer day. Not at the beach. Not at the hot springs. Not at home.

There are many injustices in the world, but with my focus on eating, I consider the worst injustice to be starvation. Given how much money goes into big business, technology, the military, political fundraising, it seems unconscionable that *one person* would starve. My version of feeding the homeless in the past didn't go so well. I was bingeing at yet another fast-food restaurant but when I walked out the door, the voice of God said, "Don't eat it. Give it to that man over there." So I did. He took one look in the bag and said, "Sorry, I don't eat junk food."

I haven't begun to help the cause yet, but find it unacceptable that anywhere in the world, people die of starvation, especially with all the money spent on weight loss medications in the world --150 billion dollars by 2035, the American Society of Health-System Pharmacists reports. I will say that I do help people address *spiritual starvation* by helping them get abstinent through my 12-step food program, but denying our excesses is a far cry from feeding people who are genuinely hungry.

In order to take care of my three grown daughters as long as possible, I eat as well as possible. Nothing goes into the body that isn't God-honoring for me. Not even on occasion. I don't ever want to eat more than my share. It bears repeating: I abstain from sugar, flour, wheat, caffeine, processed and refined foods, drink, volume, excess, and completely, not just for Lent, but always, every day, ever since November 29, 2020. Fed up with another relapse, I had prayed on November 28, "Lord, if you want me abstinent, you're just going to have to do it yourself." And he did. While he removed alcohol in 1988, somehow I never developed a drug problem other than caffeine, not even nicotine. But I qualified for the sin of gluttony with food. With the help of 12-step programs, I do not indulge. The Lord keeps me from falling from grace like Eve, resisting any original sin in the form of modern temptations. The options are around me daily, but I just pass by without partaking. This is the proper use of denial. And the proper use of the will? To lean into God.

Because the food is just food. I'm learning all about how spiritually starved I am without the Eucharist. I will be forever hungry until I experience the Eucharist for the first time. And then I will also need it the next day, and the next day after that. Right now, it is the daily missing ingredient from my soul.

I can tell how much healing is needed. For example, I thought divorce divided my soul growing up, and that I furthered the division divorcing my husband. Both are true. But the true division deep down is being separate from the Body of Christ. I might not have divorced in the first place. It's the Eucharist that is going to glue me back together. How? The Body of Christ was wounded for us, so it heals our wounds. That's what he died for, our wounds. That's why it's called a sacrifice when he died on the cross for us. It's the Body and Blood of Christ that heals our wounds. I can't heal fully without him.

Wouldn't now be a good time for you to return, Lord? How much longer do you want life here on earth to decline, especially with the existing regime in the U.S? *Lord, visions? I welcome them. If you, angels or Mary want to visit me in my dreams, I'm ready!*

How my life has changed already, looking at it through a Catholic lens. I see you, Jesus, in sharper focus. My prayers feel real and impactful. My days feel full and enough. I used to feel I wasn't doing enough or the right things, and I squandered my time. Now I'm efficient, and more responsive instantly to people. Prayerful life, I beseech thee to keep close to me and don't let even one of my thoughts fall captive to the enemy. Not one! Keep me safeguarded. Anyone who speaks with me and has a prayer is touched by your presence through me. I am dutifully yours, Lord. I love Eucharistic Adoration and how it's a resuscitator for the soul. *Thank you!*

August 2, 2025

Today as I walked in line to the front at Mass, I realized how holy that walk is, approaching the host to receive communion, even though I just cross my arms. In my case, I just want to get near it and stand before it, behold it momentarily, and look forward to the day.

What other famous walks are there in life? The wedding aisle for marriage, the green mile for the death penalty as depicted in a Stephen King novel, a school graduation aisle, funeral processions. I can't think of a more significant walk than walking down the church aisle to receive the Body and Blood of Jesus Christ every day. What a privilege. I'm just rehearsing, too. This is indeed a wedding feast of eternal magnitude. I had no idea that *come to the table* would mean all this and probably a lot more.

It just dawned on me that I'm becoming Catholic in a Jubilee year! This is significant, because it only occurs every 25 years for renewal, and I get to join in a renewal year. I'm undertaking a spiritual conversion to the true authentic religion belonging to Jesus Christ, before the reformation, which I never studied or understood. The word "jubilee" means special anniversary or event, especially one every 25 or 50 years. This is me riding the wave of conversions; it swept me up. The theme for 2025 globally is "pilgrims of hope." It's a holy year for the forgiveness of sin, conversion, and joyful celebration.

In addition to mystical moments becoming Catholic, I have moments where I want to flee Mass for no apparent reason, just run right out. I try to breathe if I can catch my already short breath. Fight or flight sets in, and it must be something subconscious lurking that just hasn't come to light yet. I must not let it chase me away.

Since June I also started giving 10 percent of my monthly income to the church, and tomorrow I don't want to give it. I just feel *greedy and needy.* I don't know what it means to be generous yet, but I'm hoping that by giving, I'll learn.

August 4, 2025

If you had an appointment with Jesus, would you be late? That is what it feels like if I'm not early or exactly on time a few moments before every Mass. Even rushing feels disrespectful, like I let cleaning the cat box come before being on time for Jesus today. Walking in late felt irreverent, almost like an expression of anger or defiance. Being early is respectful and expresses preparation, as though I have prioritized my display of affection for the

Lord. I was only late one time so far, because that one time on vacation had a profound effect on me that bad.

Today at Mass I pictured all three heavyweights – divorce, adultery and remarriage – as enemy traps, so I was able to depersonalize them. Why this shift in blame from me to Satan helps, I don't know. The enemy uses issues around money to produce doubt and insecurity, too, so just after you wade through spiritual attacks, invisible rip tides try to nab you from parallel angles.

Daily Mass treats potential sin like chlorine in a swimming pool. My dependence on it already feels like if I didn't go to Mass, I'd be pulling the plug on life support. And this is *without* experiencing the Eucharist yet. I think I was dizzy from discovering the heavyweight trio, because after I crossed my arms before the priest, I forgot where I was sitting in the pews. Catholics really watch out for each other, because a kind woman noticed right away and pointed me to my seat. It must be really obvious that I'm new. But I was so touched. I haven't met a soul yet and I like how no one approaches me because it's like they respect my space and silence and don't question why I'm there. I sent my resume to the church. I just want to get in line to work for the new church being built, volunteer *and* any paid work that would be available at the new home one day.

Today I saw online that Catholicism is its own book category on Amazon. I have much to learn about Catholic writing, and it sure will help to pick St. Francis de Sales as my patron saint. New initiates to the Catholic Church pick a patron saint. He's the patron saint of writers and journalists. To think I get my own patron saint! I heard so much negativity about Catholicism, nobody told me how fun this faith is. So I'll tell you. I've never had so much fun in a church setting in all my life. There's just so much depth and delight! I've also never been around people who were so enthusiastic about their faith.

So why am I so afraid of the priests? I thought we covered the father issues earlier. When they stand at the outdoor entrance to the church after weekend Mass to greet parishioners, I side-step them, scooting past people to take a right, hoping they don't notice I skipped the line. It isn't their personality or position that scares me; they're perfectly friendly, approachable, and most of all, accessible. It's the same unexplainable element that makes me want to run out of Mass mid-service on occasion. Plus, what do you say to a priest besides, "Hello, Father." I wouldn't even know how to have a conversation with a priest. I did ask the first priest, how do I become Catholic? That's a no-brainer of a need-to-know. I don't have anything else to say, and I'm current on my 10th steps in 12-step programs that I don't have anything to confess, nor am I Catholic yet to partake in confession. Wait, this isn't true. Didn't I just identify fear of priests?

It's that dream I mentioned earlier, not allowed into the room where the father is working. I just have this traumatic replay thing in me that doesn't feel worthy to be in their presence, which might be the same for God, too, now that I think about it. Do I feel unworthy to be in the presence of God? If so, why? I thought I dealt with this earlier. I did not have any abuse occur in religious settings, so I don't have that confusion, but I do equate "the father" with my own father abuses, so it could be as simple as that. A projection onto all other father figures. Or maybe I just need to give a good dose of Catholic forgiveness.

I read the church bulletin, and September 6 is an open house to sign up for volunteer work. I wonder what I could volunteer for now that won't overwhelm me and doesn't require being Catholic already. I had this desire to polish the pews with Lemon Pledge, but what if the church takes it as an insult that I think they're dirty, which I don't? I just loved the childhood chore of polishing wood furniture. "Offer to help clean the church" is one of the first things Stephanie suggested, but I had this crazy fear that if I volunteer, they won't hire me one day if the opportunity comes because I'll already be working for free. I have no humility yet, so while I really want to polish the pews, I can't even offer to work for them or polish for free. One thing for sure, I do not have a servant's heart yet; I'm way too selfish.

Back to the church panic. It's a flee mechanism. It's an impulse to "Go, now!" I used to get it in relationships, so it makes sense I'm getting it now with my relationship with the church, which I've chosen to make a daily relationship, day in and day out. My behaviors are just reflecting my relationship with "her" the church, and "him" our God. The desire to get out fast. Fear of intimacy. Or perhaps the ego is threatened by God's presence and wants control. It's the enemy saying, "Run, leave the body of Christ, leave the presence of the Lord." *Run!*

August 4 is heart sticker day in my family. It is the date in 2011 when my 4-year-old daughter said a famous quote that forever imprinted on my heart. And now it also explains the Eucharist! She was putting heart stickers all over my pajamas, and she put one on my heart and said: "This is God's heart. Put it on your heart and it will be food for you." So Biblical of her at age four to comprehend the heart of God as food for us, because that sums up the Eucharist in a sentence. She was baptized two years later in a Christian church. The body of Christ is God's heart, and it is the food we need, that one bite is enough to fill the entire human body with the whole body of Christ. Really ponder this. You can't learn this at the local drive-through restaurant.

There's a section on the church website, "Becoming Catholic." It says, "You are not alone," and "What is God asking of you?" He's asking me to come to the table. That is to experience his Eucharist at his table – the very table of the last supper which was really the first supper of many to come for us. On the website, it explains the stages. The main focus is on people being baptized for the first time, becoming Christian, they're called catechumens, and then the secondary but also important focus is for those who are already baptized in a Christian faith, we're called candidates. I keep saying this over and over, so it sinks in. Repetition is helping me absorb the information.

This is not an easy process. Last night I had such deep sorrow, for example, I think what I felt was God's sorrow not mine. I don't know how to explain it, but as I was watching "The Chosen" season 5 episode 8 where Jesus was in the Garden of Gethsemane praying, and he had such heartache, it somehow plunged me into my own ache from lifelong absence of the Lord. That my true loneliness and longing for the Lord will only be satisfied in the sacrament with the host.

But once I do, I will be truly fed. I used to see this same pain as unresolved grief from my life issues, but now I see it as ignoring the Lord. The conversion is changing the way I see my own past and interior life, a lack of experiencing the host, apart from the body of Christ. Thinking I'm linked to people but having no idea that I'm missing the main connecting ingredient of people – how Jesus connects us to him and his people through communion. It explains my indifference, lack of caring, and absence of empathy, selfishness, and lack of regard. Rather than me being a bad person, I am just missing the ingredient needed for my soul. How are you supposed to seek or find something you don't even know you're missing? Now I know I am missing it and lacking it, so I am preparing to receive it. I am courageous, willing to feel and face the fullness of the emptiness so I can describe it to you in full detail while I wait.

That black void inside, that endless vacuum where I sucked up food like air on binges, never could be filled no matter what I ate. If only I could have seen this earlier as a desire for God! Disciplined eating helped stage the scene to experience the vast void. I ate correctly and no more than my portion; November 2025 makes five years. I just need to hang in there for nine more months of hunger, because I have my eye on the prize now. I know that once fed, I won't feel this spiritual starvation anymore.

I wonder again, how much binge eating disorder, bulimia and anorexia or other eating disorders are a rejection or distortion of the need for the Eucharist? They all could be manifestations and distortions of not having access to the Eucharistic experience. Where are the studies and stories from people on this topic? As we all have food issues even if we don't have eating disorders, the Eucharist cannot be approached without examination of human eating habits. Because it would be hypocritical to abuse the body with food and then come before the host to receive holy communion. But also, couldn't receiving the host heal the other human eating problems, too? Once nourished in Christ, would we make better earthly eating choices?

I do feel I'm at a crossroads where if I don't seek to be spiritually nourished through the Eucharist, I am in danger of yet another relapse into my food addiction. I feel a strong desire to break abstinence right now and recall that sugar binge on the night my daughter said the "God's heart" one-liner that changed my life. But my break desire doesn't include physical hunger or craving even. It feels more like original sin calling, the enemy trying to interfere in the plan for me to receive the host, because then I will be powered by Jesus and the body of Christ, connected to other Catholics, and a real threat to the enemy.

Right now, apart from the body, I am not connected to other Catholics even though I am meeting them. I am not part of the Catholic body. As a result, I feel less connected to all other people in general. But I'm hanging out in the reality of this lost space to get a good look at it instead of ignoring it anymore. And in this detached space, I feel overwhelmed by their causes, conditions and cares, because my indifference keeps me from drowning in other people's issues. It's protective.

I knew I would be irritated easily by others because of my self-centeredness. I look forward to this changing as I become more Catholic. I'll need a tolerance to be part of other people's lives and what they go through, especially if I'm genuinely praying in response to people's prayer requests. We address them daily in Mass, the prayer of the people. Sure, I have a friendly smile, but I don't think my heart matches quite yet. But some Catholics have x-ray vision and have seen my heart of gold. *And I see such goodness in them.* These are my newfound friends.

August 5, 2025

To think there are many people who can take daily communion and choose not to, and here I must wait until April 4 next year. They're intentionally missing the fullness of their faith. Every day they could be joined in the Body of Christ to feel fortified in their daily spiritual battles at home and work.

This morning I'm thinking of Aunt Peggy. She is a devout Catholic and the sister of my stepmother Mary Ellen Mohr who abandoned her Catholicism after her parents abandoned her pregnant at 16. Aunt Peggy did not abandon her faith, even though her parents rejected her big sister, and Aunt Peggy raised her daughter Liberty as Catholic, too. I reconnected with them! We now have a host of things to talk about and catch up on. So, by marriage, I do have Catholic relatives! I have claimed them fully, as God does one of his restoration acts on the perception of lost time. I knew growing up that Aunt Peggy prayed the Rosary. I felt that she was in an untouchable, unreachable category of "devout Catholic" growing up because of the way my stepmother characterized their childhood religion as threatening. My stepmother had fallen away, but Aunt Peggy had not. Peggy always lived by her faith and didn't reject it like the other two sisters, and I don't know about their brother I never met. But this Mohr family, can you believe, is related to Joseph Mohr, the Catholic priest who wrote the words to "Silent Night," Stille Nacht. Yes! So, by marriage, I'm related to Joseph Mohr who wrote "Silent Night," though not by blood.

All I know is, there is never a dull moment in the Catholic Church. Every day is a major learning experience, challenging my intellectual abilities. And my random desires to flee now come with reasons, like today's potential job. Today I just couldn't wait even past the homily, so I missed the consecration and the communion line. Part of me thinks I'm not missing out because I can't take communion yet, but I blamed the enemy for sending me out of church early on a wild goose chase because I arrived way too early and could have stayed for all of Mass. *But this diversion by the enemy makes sense now, like an attack, because of what happened just yesterday.*

At home, resting on my couch in a sort of deep contemplative stupor, I had a vision of suddenly being at church in a pew and to my left, seated in a red king's robe with white furry collar, was Jesus himself. I could not look; I could only see the deep red robe out of the corner of my eye. I froze in awe, wait, *is this who I think it is*? The King of kings, his presence, He wasn't asking anything of me, but how could this be, because I was at home on a blue couch I got for free at the curb from outside a house near the YMCA, but we were together in the pews of The Holy Name of Jesus church on Olive Street. *There he was!* I couldn't believe he made a house call. I dared not move, once I realized who it was.

It faded in an instant, and I scrambled for my written request to verify I had asked for a vision. Sure enough, last Friday during adoration, I wrote: *"Lord, visions? I welcome them. If you, angels or Mary want to visit me in my dreams, I'm ready!"* He just sat next to me, not a word. Just appeared in the same pew right next to me.

Can't I strike up the conversation now, since I went mute during "the visit?" Here goes: Lord, thank you for visiting me yesterday. My girls won't believe it, because I'm not going to tell them. Would you speak to me as fluently and fluidly as I speak to you if I became still, silent and listened? Your presence was overwhelming enough, and to think I called for you, and you came? I welcomed a vision and got one? Dare I ask more? If you have words for me, I'll write them down.

Response: "Be at peace. Rested. Comforted. The work I have for you is each day and will be revealed slowly. You are doing enough. Don't scramble for random efforts. Let go of people and situations clearly meant for the world's expectations. In your dealings with people, do not get tangled into mental snares. Send for me. I will work on them. You are provided for. Yes, get earthquake insurance. You deserve to be heard and seen. I have people for you. Just do your best with them and give them to me. Tell your daughters about me."

Next, I interjected a question for the Lord: "How, and in what way, Lord, tell them about you?"

The response: "Through your becoming Catholic, they will see me. Let them just see me though you. Being ready, keep close to me. I am always with you to the left side. With constancy, and immediacy, seek my will on the smallest of details. I particularly put faith in your motherhood of three daughters as they need you now. I will keep you from harm and poor decisions. I will keep you safe. I will keep you healthy. I need you preserved. You will see. Trust me."

Who are you to have a private audience with the creator of the Universe? Who are you to convey words directly as if from Jesus? So barks the enemy like a rabid dog nipping at the Lord's heels. I retorted with my pen: "Because he made me, that's why. I'm his creation. I'm allowed 24/7 private access to Jesus who knows my every cell, operates my heart, breathes for me. I deserve it because I am alive. Our minds can't comprehend that Jesus does this for every human being. I deserve this privilege, honor, and duty of being alive. To ignore him would be insulting, ungrateful, and apostasy. To not acknowledge him or his presence or not try to communicate would be so sad for the maker and a lifetime of sorrow for the created being."

Everyone else has this same privilege, so it's not like I'm special or extraordinary. Everyone is a saint in the making.

August 6, 2025

John 6:53: "Truly, truly, I say to you, unless you eat of the flesh of the Son of man and drink his blood, you have no life in you."

I can tell you I know for a fact that today I do not have the life John's talking about inside my body today. *I do not know it yet.* Because even though I don't know what it feels like to have it yet, I now know that it's missing. And even though the Lord visited me yesterday, He is still not *in me* and I am still not *in him* which occurs in the moment of the Eucharistic communion.

Grace before daily meals – a task I've never mastered. Let's learn it online: "Bless us, O Lord, and these your gifts, which we are about to receive from your bounty, through Christ our Lord. Amen." And there is even prayer after the meal: "We give you thanks, Almighty God, for these and all the gifts which we have received from your goodness through Christ our Lord. Amen." It's really hard for me to remember except maybe ten bites into the meal that I forgot to pray. And one has to be really intentional to remember to pray after the meal as well. I'm going to start grace before and after meals at dinnertime today. This will grace and bless my eating and help heal any disordered elements about eating that still need a touch of grace.

If I eat slowly, spaciously, pray before and after my four meals, and plenty of water in between, I'll make it to my five-year abstinence anniversary on November 29, 2025. I usually eat these meals at 4 a.m., 9 a.m., 2 p.m. and 6 p.m. with variations on timing depending on the day's events. Breakfast is plain yogurt, milk, fruit and oat bran. Lunch is a cooked protein, salad, vegetable, olive oil and fruit. Dinner is the same plus either a baked potato or brown rice, and then comes a protein or dairy serving with a fruit in the evening. I don't eat in between, I measure all my foods to certain amounts, I only drink water, so no coffee, tea or caffeine, I don't add sweeteners or spices or condiments, snacks, tastes, bites or sips. It's heaven, this freedom. My body feels perfectly tuned to 134 pounds at 5-foot-8-½ and shrinking. I love to eat breakfast after my morning quiet time starts at 3 a.m. I attended a 12-step program for food addiction where I learned to eat this way, but we can't say Jesus in the rooms so it leaves out the primary ingredient in my food plan, which I will be eligible for on April 4, 2026.

All my eating history is leading up to this wedding feast of the Eucharist. That will be my very first Heavenly feast! Because I have made myself an empty vessel of food attachments on earth, I fully expect to be filled with the Holy Spirit! Food won't be in the way. Food won't be between me and the Lord. I just think it's so funny that bread and wine are the designated earthly elements when those are the two things I learned to abstain from all my life. They secretly contained Jesus himself! This isn't the role of 12-step programs to point this out, but it is my role now to point it out to you, should you resonate with my spiritual craving, become curious, or suffer from the same food malady.

Today I feel in limbo even though Jesus sat next to me in the vision. And every day in Mass I encounter the Body and Blood of Christ by beholding it with my eyes rather than ingesting it. I have a headache. Maybe it's from the trash compactor of emotions that the spiritual encounter emptied: Frustration, impatience, ignorance, fear, insecurity, suspicion, being fooled, feeling misunderstood, anxious, sad, left out, "where's mine?" Doubt, embarrassment, remorse, guilt, regret, angst, judgment, fear of not being in control, delight, ease, health, comfort, joy, security, and reassurance. Here comes another wave: Dislike, disregard, aloofness, unsure, unpredictable, not knowing, earthquakes, health future, financial future, "never enough," absence, serendipity, whim, spontaneity, fate, fortune, luck, choice, free will. With all this going on, no wonder we are called to holiness.

August 7, 2025

Here I was feeling shy about wanting to be a saint when it turns out it's an order of sorts that we strive to be one! I appreciate how Catholicism allows me to step in, step up, come to the table, right up close to the Lord, in him and through him, and aim for sainthood. I just don't think other churches expected this from me, so I didn't expect it from myself. I didn't know it was an option. I have a long way to go, however.

"Like the dewfall" is my favorite phrase said during Mass. I'm so close to temptation, wanting to turn to food and take the edge off this newfound feeling of being hungrier than ever. Here's the line in Mass: "Make holy, therefore, these gifts, we pray, by sending down your Spirit upon them like the dewfall." This is what invites *transubstantiation.* Like the dewfall is quiet, unseen, mysterious, life-giving, gentle. A morning person, this imagery just makes me bloom.

Today's responsorial Psalm during Mass: "If today you hear his voice, harden not your hearts." Today I am listening to the Lord's voice. My heart hardens when I'm afraid. A cold heart is a fearful one. I have a new aspiration though, because "like the dewfall" makes me want to be this very spirit when I am in the presence of people. I want them to feel that *I am like the dewfall.* Speak softly, be unseen, move quietly, slowly, carefully and with purpose, like a priest who handles the elements at the Mass with his hands. Each movement is so intentional.

August 8, 2025

For the first time in my life, I feel my prayer connects to the actual world. Don't ask me how it happens, but Mass plugs me right into the heartbeat of all humanity.

It's the all-encompassing nature of the prayers said during mass; we cover everything. And we add our own intentions in a moment at the end of the collective prayers. Day after day, this sharpens precision in identifying what and who needs prayer. I can't help but pray every day for my three daughters, and now I know they are under the care of the Mother of God, which is a great relief to my previous self-reliant Mom posture.

Eating is one of the more intimate human experiences. Actually taking something into your body that gets assimilated, becomes part of you, then eliminated. Eating junk or excess food makes no sense as far as caring about what goes into our bodies. Reverence is missing on those occasions. Copious amounts of sugar, we anesthetize the mouth, and it becomes a portal of shame and guilt. This is a sacred space. Fill it with Psalm 81:10, "Open your mouth wide, and I will fill it." Jesus, feed me! I long to be fed by you. The date is April 4, 2026. *What if I die before I get to do it?* I looked it up. If I'm close to death in a hospital, I can call for a priest and receive the sacraments just in time. That's a relief to know. Otherwise, patience is my prescription for now.

I flashed back to once as a child when a maid my mother employed took me to her church. I was freaked out by all the people crying in little heaps on the floor. The priest was laying hands on their heads one by one. It was like some Mass confession. It scared me. What were they crying about? Becoming Catholic, all my church experiences are coming back for examination as to what beliefs were formed and not formed, to distill the essence of a new truth. All my limitations show, like how I'll have to stretch to care more about other people in addition to my three daughters. I'm truly shut down right now on helping people outside my mother hen sphere. I know how to tune out the outside world, so how on earth am I supposed to tune in?

I'm especially hungry, but I think it's for the Eucharist. I'll describe how this hunger differs from ravenous, addictive, mental hunger, and true physical hunger. Mental hunger feeds on negativity, drains the mind, and stimulates the lying center of the brain that demands "more food" when physically the proper amounts of food have already been ingested. Then there's physical hunger when the body isn't getting enough of what it needs. You feel like you could be fortified.

Then there's the vacuum. This feels like a black hole carved out on the inside. It's consuming, like you could inhale, and the volume sucked in would never end. That's hunger for the Lord. The bite of the body of Christ fills the entire void where the vacuum lives. The types of hunger, if you can distinguish among them, contain their own instructions on how to not feed the wrong one. Mental hunger requires truth, physical hunger requires food, and spiritual hunger requires the Eucharist.

August 9, 2025

Right now, temptation for eating binge foods and drinking coffee is at an all-time high, of course because my Catholic classes begin in two weeks and the enemy wants to trip me on the way there, starting now. Always lures with the same foods, too. The best lie the enemy uses is: "You know Jesus will still forgive your sins *if you just do it this once.*" The enemy twists the unconditional nature of the love of God as a justification for sinning. The logic is mind boggling, because it makes sense in the dishonest moment. I won't fall for it. I eat the way I do *because I love God.* If I wanted to serve the enemy, I'd be making the rounds bingeing right now and they'd know my name again at Starbucks.

My goal is to make it through the next two weeks without sabotage. My personality feels flattened, deadened, dulled, as if I lack clarity or fell into a fog where caffeine and sugar are required to see again. They're not.

Lord, touch my mind! Sharpen it! Touch me with your brilliance to break this mental lockdown. Lord, thank you. I have gratitude for: A relationship with you, financial wellbeing, good health and abstinence, security and safety, a two-hour daily writing ritual, daily Mass, my breath, physical mobility, home space, and all three daughters. Amen! Now is the time to lean into the host and ignore all food thoughts or just use them as a cue to trust God more, seek deeper, and dive into blank books letting the ink create an anchor. Maybe I'm to withstand temptation now as I write this so that by the time you read this, I will help you not give into your temptations, either. Let me help you by asking: Do you eat in a God-honoring way? I do, but it's not easy. You have to say "no" politely all the time. Soon you learn you don't have to give reasons, either.

This was my grandmother's birthday in 1907. She would clutch her rosary lying in bed after her stroke. Now it seems like she was more Catholic than Episcopal, this woman who insisted on my baptism. She was scary, but I loved her because my mother loved her. She never told my mother she loved her or even hugged her, I'm told. I heard Grandmum was sexually abused by an uncle and brother. The time to deal with secrets is now. We can't hide from the Lord. A heavy smoker and drinker, Grandmum was a walking contradiction. Prayers from her were stinky with smoke and alcohol. I wanted nothing to do with prayer, so I held my breath.

Today at Mass then adoration afterward, I felt separation anxiety to the point of tears. The idea of leaving church once I got there, I felt like a baby being left at childcare, only it was me coming and going from the mother, church. What if the "exit panic" I feel is separation anxiety I feel in my relationship with the Lord? Fear of abandonment? There was something touching about discovering I might have separation anxiety from Jesus and his Mother Mary, or is it "her," the church overall? I don't know enough about this new dynamic.

Meanwhile, here is a version I found of the Spiritual Communion Prayer for me to say each Mass, while not participating in communion. It's on page 144 of Matthew Kelly's book, *33 Days to Eucharistic Glory*: "Jesus, I believe that you are present in the Most Holy Sacrament of the Eucharist. Every day I long for more of you. I love you above all things, and I desire to receive you into my soul. Since I cannot receive you sacramentally at this moment, I invite you to come and dwell in my heart. May this spiritual communion increase my desire for the Eucharist. You are the healer of my soul. Take the blindness from my eyes, the deafness from my ears, the darkness from my mind, and the hardness from my heart. Fill me with the grace, wisdom and courage to do your will in all things. My Lord and my God, draw me close to you, nearer than ever before. Amen.

How close can I get to the Eucharist without taking communion? This is my mission for the next nine months. I'll look at it like going from conception, first forming in the womb, to live birth. With this symbolism, I get to become a cradle Catholic *as an adult.*

I recalled today what first piqued my curiosity in the Catholic Church. One Sunday in the Baptist church, we were prompted to pray for people who were "Roman

Catholics, who worship saints and idols." Not sure how I knew that to be untrue of Catholicism, so I wondered if Roman Catholic meant something else, so I decided to investigate by seeing for myself.

August 11, 2025

When first exploring the idea of communion, and rejecting the idea to preserve my food abstinence, I claimed that my four abstinent meals were communion enough with the Lord. That would be my justification for not taking the wafer and wine. That was a step in the right direction, because it was me embracing all the food as God-honoring, and it expressed my desire to honor God, misguided as it was. Because I still didn't see the Eucharist as the body of Christ. Curiosity was sparked in the Scripture of John 4:32, "I have food to eat of which you do not know." Then Jesus continues in verse 34: "My food is to do the will of him who sent me, and to accomplish his work."

The Eucharist is the food I didn't know about, coming with an instruction that we perform his will and do his work. When I put two and two together, I saw how the consecrated host is separate from my earthly food; He isn't *in my food.* By eating the Blessed Sacrament, *I am in him.* I still have a question whether the consecrated host still contains the properties of bread. But I don't have gluten intolerance or Celiac's disease. If it does trigger my bodily cravings, I can ask the priest about the low-gluten alternative. If cravings develop, especially if I ingest it every day, I still don't have to act on the cravings generated. God will give me grace.

My personal pilgrimage through the book Stephanie sent me, *33 Days to Eucharistic Glory,* starts in three days so that it will end on September 14 with the Exaltation of the Holy Cross. The Catholic precision with dates is right up there with my love for dates and significant occasions.

Lord, what do you want me to do for the Catholic Church first? This morning, I envisioned collecting people's stories of their time spent in Adoration. My mission now for these 33 days: How close can I get to the Lord without taking the Eucharist? I can only go so far without it. So the pilgrimage is to come up as close as I can, as if I am hand to mouth distance away every day. Shore up all the space between me and the table. How vast is that land? Is it miles, years, ages, or eons? Is it even visible or tangible, calculable? How far am I away from the table even? I cannot tell. I just know I want to be face to face with God and not wait until I get to Heaven.

Today with the active food addicts I talk to regularly on the phone, I feel short-tempered and impatient. I'm dealing with people who obviously don't want to quit their binge foods even though they know they're supposed to. I think I'll use a couple of Jesus's lines next time, borrowing from the paralyzed man at the spring: "Do you want to get well?" You'd think the answer would be "of course," but their lack of action is the true lie detector test.

In the food recovery programs, there is lots of relapse into disordered eating, more than there are people recovering from it. I often feel outrage about the relapse because our official primary purpose is to abstain and help others abstain. People aren't willing to suffer up front by saying, "I want to break it but won't." They come for help afterward, saying "I broke it," having suffered on their own. If they had asked for help, they might have experienced grace. Imagine if Eve had sought God out and said, "Help me, Lord, Satan is tempting me!" That's how I was; I knew if I asked for help, I might receive it, and then not get to eat the desired items.

This lack of commitment to remain abstinent reminds me of my failure to keep committed to my marriage that ended in 2008. It isn't like my continued commitment to food abstinence is going to bring back the marriage, but it explains why I react poorly to people breaking their food commitments to abstinence. All my broken food commitments were really a symptom of my broken marital commitment through divorce. God had to put an end to the lie that I need to re-enact breaking commitments all over the place to replay original sin.

Addictions to flour (bread) and wine (alcohol) for me are distortions of the need for the Eucharist, distorted manifestations resulting from the absence of the Eucharist. Now I'm starting to find the words to articulate my experience, repetitive as I'm being. In the Eucharist, God nourishes us and becomes part of our cells.

Ordered eating could be described as bringing God into our relationship with food and our eating. So what happens when we eat poorly, then come before God asking to receive his holiness, after we have so poorly fed his body temple? I read online, "For Catholics, the Eucharist is the food that satisfies our hungry desires for heaven. The Eucharist is what sustains our spiritual life here on earth." In that case, no wonder I'm starving without it. That's why it looks like banana bread, cookies and coffee are going to hit the spot. But it will only increase the distance between me and the Lord if I choose that again. Excess = emptiness. The Eucharist preserves, increases and renews the life of grace received at baptism, separates us from sin, and preserves us from future mortal sins. (CCC 1392-3 and 1395). CCC is this lovely handful of a white book Stephanie sent me, the Catechism of the Catholic Church.

This explains why I attend Mass daily and have to settle for this temporary "Spiritual Communion Prayer" in the meantime. I say it daily at Mass in lieu of consuming the consecrated host. I'm grasping to understand: *Our presence within his body is more important than his presence in us.* Without it, we can't fulfill our vocations! This sacrament connects us to the source of all grace and holiness, and the more we receive it, the stronger our connection becomes.

Before I start my *33 days to Eucharistic Glory* on August 14, I want to set aside my frustration issues with active food addicts, and obsession over seeking used cars and searching job openings. They can't be issues. Lord, I'm having trouble discerning why I keep being guided to sell my car. I would feel much safer in the world if I didn't drive. The deep desire in my heart is not to drive for a while, hence the recurring dreams of *potential* car crashes, all averted. And I know enough to know that if I don't surrender to something that is God's will, it gets taken in one way or another, potentially unfavorably, as a consequence for resisting nudges meant for my good. The saying we are punished by our sins, not for them, also applies to we are punished by our inaction when we are guided to act.

Today I realized *the gift* the first priest prayed over for me is the calling to share the truth of the glory of God through the Eucharist. It's much easier to protect a gift when you know what it is. Through the lens of the Catholic Church, my life has come into sharper focus. I'll be able to help people much better with their divorce urges and food urges. Until then, it's all about keeping close to God by skirting the enemy; just go the opposite direction of where he points.

This is a good time to remind myself again what this hunger looks, acts and feels like in spiritual starvation mode, so that I have something to compare it to after April

4, 2026. I feel spiritually starved, completely abstinent from unholy eating, but completely without the Eucharist. The Eucharist is our food for the journey home, today's manna from heaven. It makes sure we are connected to the source of all holiness and spiritual strength. It isn't enough that Jesus is in me in spirit, I have to be in him in the way he said to abide in him through the Eucharist. In the Spiritual Communion Prayer, I'm getting a full dose of the line: "May this spiritual communion increase my desire for the Eucharist." I just don't want any more desire for it. I have enough desire for an army of new converts. I wonder if it's contagious. If so, how do I spread it while I'm waiting?

August 12, 2025

Women aren't priests in the Catholic Church but they can be saints, something priests can also aspire to. So, let's understand before jumping to judgment: Jesus was a man, and therefore priests are men because they are meant to embody Jesus for us when they step into his role at the last supper ever Mass all over the world. Respecting this reasoning doesn't make it sexist.

Today the visiting priest said at my turn in line with my arms crossed: "May the Lord make you an instrument of his love." And this was a religion to fear? The enemy attacks, giving people trouble with Catholicism – it appears to them as something wrong with the religion when it's the thinking about the religion that is the trouble. *This is a beautiful religion.* It's so quiet in my home right now as I write, it's like I brought the Eucharistic adoration home with me. The stillness inside is like a deep pond.

It's clear the enemy doesn't want me Catholic! Now that I know this, I want to be Catholic more than ever. And since Jesus already overcame the enemy, it isn't my fight with the enemy, but my effort to dwell within the shelter of the one who already won.

I can tell the enemy is trying to sabotage my attendance at Catholic classes next week by getting me to sell my car. I won't fall for it, or the enemy's other tactics: other people's opinions, doubt, confusion, fear, distractions, and the same old binge foods and drinks I've gone without active food addiction for almost five years now. I keep saying it to reinforce the truth that God's grace over that is greater than any temptation.

AI spells out how the enemy tries to block participation in Catholicism, leading people away from God and salvation with: "Excessive attachment to worldly goods, pride, sinful behaviors, fears of church teachings, concerns about sin or guilt, doubts about the validity of the faith, trauma from past experiences, misconceptions and negative stereotypes." *Don't fall for it.*

Faced with prayer, personal reflection and discernment, fellowship, community, education and study, none of these elements must interfere. If other people's opinions were the guiding factor, I would have to sacrifice my personal relationship with the Lord for *the conditions of the world.* One person feared I would switch political parties. (Right now in the USA, 33 percent of Catholics are Democrats and 28 percent are Republican and 30 percent are neither.) Another said I should join the Episcopal Church in fairness to homosexuality. *I can't let people's opinions on what the church stands for come before my own personal conviction in the true presence of the Lord.* It doesn't make me prejudice against homosexuals just because I want to experience Jesus in the Holy Sacrament of the Eucharist.

August 13, 2025

On pilgrimage day one of *33 Days to Eucharistic Glory* by Matthew Kelly, I'm off to a horrifying start. It's the darkness that came out of left field that demands *reader discretion advised*:

I got a whiff of the sacramental wine on the breath of the visiting priest who said to me at my turn in line: "May you be an instrument of his wonderful love." I hadn't even returned to the pew before the whiff transported me back in time to age six, lying in bed pretending I was asleep while drunk artists peered over the sleeping angel-child me, oohing and ahhing thinking they weren't waking me.

My mother, Mary, always wanted to show them how I slept with both hands over my heart like a princess. That image flashed back to three years earlier when my parents' "friend" stayed the night, snuck into my room to molest me and the child in the next bed. *I thought we were being eaten alive.* How do I convey the *monstrosity* of feeling at age three like you're being eaten alive? Such disgust hides behind a wheat wafer.

I expected a holy and exhilarating start to a 33-day journey with spiritual confetti, bells and whistles, and instead, welcome back to the worst nightmare of childhood. This is what I have to bring to the table, or else be hindered by it, and not get my holy moment with Jesus in April. This is all starting to feel like the real premarital counseling I should have been doing with my one and only marriage in 1992. Who knew this would replicate marriage counseling on a large scale by joining a church? Plus, I thought I asked the abuser to leave and now he's back again, maybe for that forgiveness I mentioned earlier.

Not only that, but there was also some schism in the sound system at church this morning before Mass, a giant, startling slurping sound I was certain was Satan making an appearance just for me, as if reminding me he's on the pilgrimage with me. *"You think this will be easy for you? I'm coming along for the ride."* Perhaps "schism" is too harsh a word for technology. A schism is defined as "a split or division between strongly opposed sections or parties, caused by differences in opinions or beliefs."

Sooner or later, we must face buried trauma from childhood if we are going to become Catholic. There's no way around it. Because there's no denying abuse with wounds that are also all spiritual in nature. All physical abuse is also spiritual abuse, because it affects our trust, especially in God. I'd like to think God protects me from humans simply because I ask for protection, but there is so much abuse of human life where humans aren't protected, I think instead that God doesn't prevent us from hurting each other. I would like to believe God can protect us from hurting each other. But he didn't stop me from ruining my family with divorce, so maybe I'm still angry at God for not saving my marriage, yet another element to bring to the table for inspection.

The 33-day pilgrimage with Kelly's book will end with me being officially consecrated to the Eucharist, even though I don't officially get to receive it. I'm "set apart" for the task to receive it! The overall journey examines some heavy-duty questions I decided to answer (in italics) on day one:

Who am I? *Child of God.*

Where did I come from? *The heart of God.*

What am I here for? *To share his heart.*

How do I do it? *By writing.*

Where am I going? *Home to be with God again.*

Life itself is the pilgrimage. We are here for a short time. I need to make it count. Every day counts. A short answer is better than no answer, but sometimes we have to just live out the questions until answers come. And let the answers keep changing as needed.

There is so much contemplation involved in being Catholic, I can hardly keep up. Today I thought, what if one day people could just look in my (blue) eyes and see the love of God? What if my eyes could reveal my heart, his heart? People would look at my eyes but see and feel Christ. Is that possible? What would I need to do to clear my eyes and heart for that to happen? Lately there is a fog before me, even at Mass this morning, and a cloud over my heart. But that will be my goal: To visibly show God's love from my heart through my eyes. Maybe I can find the saint for vision. Ah, there she is online! Meet Saint Lucy. *St. Lucy, clear my heavenly vision, grant me visions in this world of that world, that I might glorify my Father in Heaven, on earth.* I'm thinking this is a noble goal that will require me staring into the host whenever there is adoration. That's the ministry I'll volunteer for first at church – first Friday Adoration!

August 14, 2025

Day two of the Kelly reading, I determined I am a pilgrim and not a tourist through life. My mom was a tourist, reaching and grabbing for as many experiences and possessions as she could pack in. I rejected materialism. After my parents divorced in 1974 they lived into their 80s and 90s still holding grudges over money fought over from the past. I participated in the greed to keep their love. When they both died within three years of each other, I felt liberated from their grudges.

As a pilgrim, I'm defined by the dictionary as "a person who journeys to a sacred place for religious reasons." Every day I go to Mass, it's a pilgrimage to The Holy Name of Jesus church. One future day, it will be just half a mile from my house at the new location, 1551 E. Lugonia Avenue, now a giant empty lot under construction.

For now, each day I make a pilgrimage to 115 W. Olive Avenue in Redlands for spiritual communion each day with the Body and Blood of Christ, awaiting physical communion next April 4. It's the most important event and meal of every day, and it's complete by 8 a.m. weekdays. Now I can't see ever going without it, even though I've only feasted my eyes upon it.

I have that *newbie energy* that can annoy people and even suggests potential burnout, like a fast-fading comet. Even though I've met people who are genuinely inspired by my newcomer enthusiasm, I fear I'm joining a community where I won't fit. A deep unworthiness exists in me to fully participate in the human experience, ever since I failed at marriage.

Who cares? Next topic: This day honors the Blessed Virgin Mary being assumed body and soul into Heaven at the end of her earthly life. Nothing like the Virgin Mary to take one's eyes off oneself. The Catholic faith will make me a selfless person one day, I'm sure of it. This is part of my conversion process.

Of course, Satan has to attack again, and this time picked my white man shame complex, just applying for a job with the local tribe: *"You can't become Catholic because they abused Native Americans converting them."* With so many hot spots and triggers in this church, maybe it's one of the reasons Jesus said it's easier for a camel to get through the eye of a needle than for someone to enter the kingdom of God. I see no room for sin, slack or error, if one is to remain holy. Keep in mind I know nothing about the Catholic sacrament of reconciliation yet, other than it stands for confession. But I know from the food usage of my past that I can't be using God's potential forgiveness as a justification to depart from holiness. For now, I am free from all fleshly strongholds, Lord, thank you!

Everything in life has more meaning now. I long to see life through a long, sharp, focused Catholic lens, and look through the eyes of the Lord. Today's virtue in the Kelly book is joy, asking me: How do I embody the joy of the Lord apart from what does or doesn't happen in this life? My work right now is becoming Catholic, to find out.

August 15, 2025

Day three, the virtue of the day in Kelly's book is faith. Do people who receive the body of Christ truly feel satisfied? I'm convinced it's the missing element from my life, and I'll only experience true satisfaction once receiving Eucharist for the first time. No food on earth would make me want to give up this pursuit of the Heavenly meal. In my first book, I complained about not having God in my body. Now that I know there's a way to do it that I never knew about before, I don't want to risk losing or missing this opportunity.

Enter this holy space known as the body temple. Do not put in junk food, chemicals, or drugs. Eat in a holy manner. What does that look like to you? Do not defile your taste buds, your senses. Shield yourself. What does that look like to you? I don't want to come to this table alone. I want to bring a flock of you with me, those of you with every type of eating disorder, binge eaters, sugar addicts, caffeine addicts, food addicts, obese, anorexic, dysmorphia, alcoholics, anyone with an eating or drinking disorder, especially the *spiritually starved.*

I submit to you that your disorder could be a malformation of the needs and desires for the Holy Eucharist. No matter your religion, still come to the table for light to be shed upon your eating disorder. *Let the Eucharist rearrange it.*

My words have form, substance, contain divinity, they are drops of the Holy Spirit people will eat like morsels. I will feed them with my words in the spirit of one of my favorite Proverbs, 25:11 : “A word fitly spoken is like apples of gold in a setting of silver.” I can see this book. It ends before the Eucharist is even received. The book is all about getting ready. What’s involved in getting ready? What don’t I know that I need to know in order to become Catholic? We’ll find out. I’m a voice of ignorance shouting to the world to come to the table with me. In this liminal space between heaven and earth *I have been given grace as if the Eucharist has already been received.* This is a space of connection and protection until First Communion.

Come to the table, all who are burdened and heavy laden, with crosses to bear, axes to grind, set them down. Have a seat. Be quiet. Sit for a moment before the Lord. Let his presence move you to tears for no reason at all. Don’t stress to interpret why, don’t even text someone on your phone. Just sit and feel the relief, the love before you waiting to envelope you in its wondrous ways. Let the Holy Spirit have its way with your heart. Where do the tears come from? We don’t analyze, criticize, or interpret. We just weep. Because God knows, so we don’t have to know. Here is an app to find your nearest Catholic Church including adoration times: www.Masstimes.org Steal away to a Catholic Church; don’t let your life run away with your faith.

Turning Catholic, it feels like God is less mine alone, and more “Our Father.” Before, it’s as though I had God to myself, but now I have God out in the world. Because there's so much to do within the Catholic Church, it also would be too easy to feel like you're never doing enough, especially when you start to see the rest of your life through this Catholic lens. I've been really under-utilizing my experience, talents and abilities, now that I see how much more I'm capable of with the help of the Holy Spirit.

August 16, 2025

Saturday Adoration

Day Four in Kelly's book is on determination. Being a purposeful pilgrim with my eye on Heaven, I can set aside the distractions of this world and focus on what's important. There's a lot more that goes into becoming Catholic than they tell you on the church website or that Stephanie and I can pack into our hour-long weekly talks.

This is the message that today's reading conveyed to me: *You will be attacked by the enemy on all sides and on all fronts at all hours.* Just to be ready for what I'll call the resistance to becoming in closer relationship to God. But consider this italicized warning a compliment when it happens, because it means that you're *so on to the truth* that Satan is after you. It's a validation, because if it weren't the truth you were finding, you wouldn't be a threat, so you wouldn't be worth the enemy's time. You'd think Satan would be tired of using coffee against me, because all I've done for five years is drink water in the face of temptation. He's just waiting for the one time I give in.

Today I watched the movie "Spotlight" again and determined that human sin within the Catholic Church doesn't make Jesus any less real in Body and Blood, Soul and Divinity, in the Holy Eucharist. I know one Catholic woman who was sexually abused by a priest after her husband died, who said a worse abuse would have been had she let him drive her away from the Catholic Church and the Eucharist. He was defrocked, and Catholic Charities paid for two years of her therapy.

I can't let other people's experiences or sinful human behavior at large determine my belief system for me. I had to learn to not evaluate Jesus by human behavior. My faith in the Lord does not depend upon how man behaves. It once did. But I was wrong to blame God for man's deeds. Now if I could learn not to evaluate Jesus by what does or doesn't happen to the people I love or people in general, we'd have a better relationship, he and I. But I still evaluate Jesus by what does or doesn't happen to other people.

Today a Saint Maria Goretti relic visited the church as part of the Jubilee celebration. I brought my favorite pen, a red Palm Springs International Film Festival pen, to touch the relic. I didn't have a rosary to bring. That makes my pen a third-class relic itself, by touching a saint's personal belonging. I got to the front of the line and the woman handing out cards for the occasion saw my pen and said, "Remember who you're writing to." It put the fear of God in me. Am I writing *to* God, or *for* God, or *to* people, or *for* people, or for myself? In my instant paralysis, I couldn't touch my pen to the relic, so I don't even think it got its third-class ranking. Instead, I presented my pen before the relic. Being inches from a sacred Catholic relic felt so mysteriously powerful, there was no need for my comprehension.

St. Maria Goretti, a young girl who died five years before my grandmother was born, was murdered. She's famous for her forgiveness of the perpetrator which led to his conversion. A patron saint to teens and protection of purity, I could have benefitted from her patronage growing up. As I studied the saint on my phone from my pew, I decided to get back in line and do it right this time. I whispered to the same wise woman, "I'm writing to Jesus," and she said, "Amen." I'm not writing for the world or to the world but *to and for* the Lord only! So, when I touched the card and my pen to the relic, I pushed it by accident, making the live uniformed human guards on both sides of the relic momentarily nervous. The shift in "writer consciousness" for me was like an earthquake.

I got back to my seat. This may not seem epic to you but let me provide some context: This is my Palm Springs International Film Festival pen where I work on this "since 2010" screenplay "Fault Line." Shifting the relic suddenly revealed the symbolism of my earthquake screenplay was lacking: *The fault line has to do with the line between sin and no sin. Holiness!* Now I think I can develop a plot line. It's been dragging for fifteen years. My only deadline on this script is "the big one." My film would be pointlessly produced after a big quake.

What if Jesus is my only audience? I never ever once thought about a book as writing *to or for* Jesus, even though I've written many personal letters to him. As writers, we're supposed to consider our target audience. In the last book, it was "married couples with children who are on the verge of divorce." But Jesus? This changes everything about writing. We're not talking channeling; God needs no one to speak for him. I'm writing to the Lord, declaring my love for him, honor of him, and proclaiming his glory. I'm simply responding to his invitation to come to the table with my words, when I write two hours a day. *I'm writing this book to him.*

Meanwhile, as a result of all this veneration, I wrote to my brother today to forgive him of a debt I perceived he owed me. Just now in church I sent the email right from the pew. I had to, because this saint's birthday is July 6, the same birthday as my brother in 1957, so I knew Saint Maria was asking me to forgive him.

We come to the table multiple times every day for our earthly food. We bring ourselves in whatever condition we are in at the moment, to eat, to be fed. We love to eat, and some of us would never dream of missing a meal. But there is one meal I've missed every day of my 59 years on earth, and that's the Lord's Supper. While we pass our time on earth, we get to have our heavenly meal, too. At first it sounded creepy and cannibalistic, but that's because my sexual abuse issues were haunting me. Why would we need the Body and Blood of Christ here and now? Why don't we all wait until we get to Heaven? Precisely! It's because we are on earth that makes this heavenly meal so special.

Before I could even think of taking communion, I had to clear up the confusion between biological father and Heavenly Father. One is my parent, and the other is God. And God wasn't to blame for my father's sin. My father could have gone to confession at any church in the San Diego diocese if he were Catholic, and said to a priest, "Forgive me father for I have sinned." He had options to deal with his sin. As it is, his guilt drove him to live 3,000 miles away with another wife. Anyway, just knowing he could have gone to confession helps me separate the abuse from God. To understand that Jesus also died for the sin of my father against me, also helps me forgive my father.

Hard work aside, I had no idea that formal religion could be so fun! I imagined everyone before in spiritual straight jackets. It's fascinating, interesting, full of daily miracles just by the alertness it provides through its lens on the world. Catholic prayer is so effective against the enemy's attacks. Look up the Saint Michael Archangel Intercessory Prayer. Satan is uninventive, predictable, unresourceful, repetitive, and most of all, petty. Plus, I must always remember that the enemy has already been defeated.

My biological mother Mary, bless her heart, firmly asserted her belief in "I love humanity, but I hate people." I knew that to be true, because she hated my father the most. I don't know if Albert Einstein quoted Edna St. Vincent Millay or if she quoted him, but they agreed with my mom. Albert: "I love humanity, but I hate humans." And Edna: "I love humanity, but I hate people." You hear enough of this growing up and you grow up with the principle that people are to be hated. My attitude toward humanity is one to overcome if I'm going to become Catholic.

I'd like to have my heart changed by April, thank you Lord, so that when I receive communion, my heart is worthy of John 13:34: "A new commandment I give to you, that you love one another; even as I have loved you, that you also love one another."

My mom really did hate people by the way, even her children that she also loved most. Such contradictions constrict the heart, contort it, and twist love. Because this too is how her father behaved. She told me, "He hated his kids," third person, as if trying to separate herself from the equation, as I just did in the sentence before. Lord, empty the hate from my heart, any generational hate while you're at it, and let me embrace your sacred heart.

I thought this pen was out of ink but I started writing after veneration and found there was a lot of ink left for my two hours today. From now on, I'll be writing *to Jesus* two hours a day – just based on that one Catholic woman's one sentence. I'll have to find out her name. I see her at

Mass all the time. I wonder if I could also change someone's life in a sentence.

August 17, 2025

Day five of the pilgrimage book: fear of missing out. And five more days until OCIA starts. I read in Kelly's book that consecration liberates us from all the distraction and superficiality of the culture and names what's important. On page 36, "Consecrating yourself and your life to Jesus in the Eucharist is a serious thing. It will be uncomfortable at times, but it will also bring you spiritual gratification like none you have ever known before now."

This is already true! I've been almost three months into my Catholic journey and even my body is physically changing. I did drop weight unintentionally somehow, I feel more solid in my flesh, grounded, more substantial, more visible. I won't be getting lost in religion with what I'm finding. I'm learning to be more honest.

Luckily, loving people doesn't require liking them, so I'm forever off the hook and can now rise to the occasion. Example: I loved my mother deeply, but never liked her. Luckily with my daughters, I love them and like them. I'd be so disappointed if my daughters loved me but didn't also like me. I felt a tinge of that prospect by turning Catholic: *What if the girls won't like me when I'm Catholic?* Or what if being Catholic alienates them from me? I'll have to take this risk to improve my relationship with Jesus.

All I know is, I'm called to be a holy, good person, and to show up daily, both at the table of the Mass and to the table where I write.

August 18, 2025

I volunteered to be part of the First Friday Adoration ministry, which means I get to be a sort of guardian of the adoration for an assigned hour. I'm simply sitting in the presence of God for one hour. I've never been given such an easy task, so holy, so simple, so pure. This would be really hard to miss or mess up. Perfect commitment for my stage of becoming Catholic.

August 20, 2025

I woke up at 3 a.m. and purposely requested a vision before going back to sleep. I dreamt of a triptych, which is art in three sections, and it appeared three times like in flashes before I could grasp the image on the third appearance. "Oh, that's Mary!" I say of the Holy Mother, an image of her depicted over the newsprint, situated above a beautiful bright blue pool of holy water spanning the three tapestries, calling upon my love for natural hot mineral springs.

If I were an artist, I would create this triptych of Mary and the pools right now! How holy it felt to have a dream of Mother Mary and holy water on the day before I begin my official classes. I felt blessed all day. Didn't I just write the other day about feeling like a "deep pond" inside? It's like the three sections represent the trinity. I'll learn all about it in OCIA.

Then the dreamed shifted to a vision of the current Holy Name of Jesus church over in the new location, but with an ornate front that seemed way fancier than our modern artist renderings at church. *It was a church in Heaven* already right there on the new land.

When I asked Father Arinze how to become Catholic, I told him how I live half a mile from the new church. He said: “God is building it just for you.” I felt so special! That kind of personal touch is what I like. It felt so welcoming. And I already thought it was a cue to go there when I first discovered it. Like finding the church that day on vacation around the corner from my hotel. Like finding out Catholics all over the world are on the same page in churches about what they read and celebrate. Like all messages originating from the same readings on the liturgical calendar. I like this uniformity.

Classes start tomorrow night for the Order of Christian Initiation for Adults at The Holy Name of Jesus Catholic church in Redlands, California. I fully anticipated any potential sabotage getting to and from my first class, so even reloaded my Lyft app.

The sacraments in this religion will draw me closer to God and people. In the end, and in the beginning, it’s all about people. Like that cute hand game we played as children: “Here’s the church, here’s the steeple, open the doors and there’s all the people.” I will learn about people now. God’s people. How he wants me to love others, and better. There will be a group of us in the class where we will join the journey to becoming Catholic. Stephanie already said she would fly from Boston to California for my initiation. It will be our first meeting in person.

My becoming Catholic will also have a greater impact on me being of service. I can model myself after the saints. They make me want to be a better person, a holier person. And to have a greater impact on people in my world. And to learn more what it means to follow the Lord in my life now. Because in the end, my most important relationship on earth is the one with the Lord. It determines the quality of all my human relationships.

For the last two days, Satan has dredged up my father’s and the “family friend’s” abuses, what, as reasons not to become Catholic? To confuse me into thinking the church will repeat my past rather than help me repent from lifelong resentments over them? How ridiculous. The very fact that trauma is in my face as I enter the door of the Catholic Church is proof God is trying to heal it. This is exactly the juncture I abandoned my marriage in 2008, so I'm only returning to the issues I left behind.

How to articulate this journey is complicated. Should I write a daily diary? Will you be bored? Will it be TMI? Will I die of shame and overexposure? Will I embarrass anybody or myself? "Remember who you're writing to," said the witness to my third-stage relic pen initiation when we had the Saint Maria Goretti mini-monstrance visitation.

When I write to "you" the perceived audience, we all go off track. When I direct it to the Lord, we are all found. Lord, steer me clear of the potholes, pitfalls, and pathos plaguing me left and right. Lord, put blinders on Satan so it can't see me or find me because I'm so hidden in your glory – so Satan doesn't even have eyes for me or ears for me, it can't detect me anymore. I am not on its radar even. Just like the enemy used to never be on mine.

I am now so protected that Satan doesn't even know where to look for me. I suddenly feel like I'm inside the Sanctuary and the doors have shut on Satan outside. I yell through the closed doors: "Get thee hence!" I might have to repeat it. This feels true for the moment. If I know anything about this journey, it's a constant vigil. There's a reason vigilance includes the word vigil. I've never had to be more watchful in my entire life. I can see why it would be so much easier *not to become Catholic.* But that would mean never experiencing the Eucharist. And now that I know what I'm missing, missing it is agonizing. I've found the real source of all my cravings in life that manifested themselves into endless distortions. I can't go back.

My goal: To not let anything come in between me and my first communion next spring.

So far, Catholics are the friendliest religious people I've ever met. The very first friendliest Catholic I met in life was my sister's husband Tom. They married in 1990 and I was in their wedding as Maid of Honor, a real Catholic Mass wedding ceremony at the University of San Diego. Always enthusiastic and active, he went to Mass daily, and adored my sister. He came from a big family where they all seemed to interact. The word is "wholesome." That's what stood out.

It's the people *who don't like Catholics* who are the unfriendly ones. Their tongues can be so sharp, you make a silent decision to strategize how not to become a target in the future. One such person discovered I was becoming Catholic and immediately attacked, suggestion another church. Too late, I had already discovered Catholics believe the Eucharist is really the Body of Christ, not just a symbol. Too late, I had already seen Christ in the Eucharist for myself, what need would there be to go somewhere else? Sometimes I can't contain my joy in becoming Catholic, but quickly learned how irritating this is for some people. Then I have to reign in any evil desire to purposely upset them with my jubilance, as that would just delight Satan.

I find people's reactions to my becoming Catholic so fascinating, so I'm starting to share about my conversion project openly wherever I go. While I proudly announce it with the excitement of getting a new job, the general response is looking down, signaling it could be any number of silent reasons. Either way, I have triggered the silent reflex. No one has yet to ask why I'm so excited about it, but when I volunteer that I get to take my first communion next April and feel like I'm getting married, they look as puzzled as someone who can't find the missing game piece.

But you should see the other Catholics light up when I tell them I'm new. Not only do they know what I'm talking about, *they also know what I don't know yet.* They're excited for what they know is in store for me, that I don't know about yet. And their anticipation for me is half the fun. They're all like the precious beads on a rosary: keepers!

I'm building a foundation of religion for the first time. It feels like my life is in suspension, lifted up by God's grace, so he can slip the new foundation underneath me now at 59. But while it's up in the air, unnecessary stuff is falling away from me left and right, being shaken off, dismantled. Whatever he doesn't want on the foundation will drop off and fall away. People, activities, memories, thought processes, attachments, objects, possessions, old ways. You name it. Each day adds a new stick to the nest.

At church tonight, "Dwell" is a midweek adoration occurring monthly in honor of the Jubilee year. It's so fitting for me to have one right before my Catholic classes begin tomorrow. Like Christmas Eve is to Christmas. Reverence in the Catholic Church is even more profound than I expected it would be. Night is a mentally sloppy time for me when visions would likely never occur. The intellect is sharpest and keenest around 3 a.m., sometimes even 2 a.m., and 4 a.m. feels late these days. Yes, the 2 a.m. to 4 a.m. time frame is my favorite time of day. I once ran a club called Early Risers International in the 1990s; why did I ever end it? I really wish I stuck with the club. Visions or dreams that are profound usually occur after I awaken at those early hours, but then fall back asleep to dream before dawn. I just noticed a big "P" on the tabernacle. I never saw it before. Or is that a sword handle?

Lord, you are the best contact lens ever! Thank you for the past 50 years since my baptism, but the next 50 years are all yours now. I think life was all about me for the last 50 years. My life expectancy being 106, 50 makes it 109, but it's niftier to say 50 down, 50 to go, so what's a little exaggeration on my life expectancy. Everything seems possible here in front of the Eucharist. Here, my mind won't go anywhere without you, Lord. It's all you, here on out. I've never had so much hope and so much freedom from fear in my heart, no tugs of selfishness except for what the enemy tried to pull today, but I didn't fall for it or indulge because I knew it was about me starting class tomorrow.

Lord, it's nice to be around all these people who adore you like I do and just want to be in your presence because it's so magnificent. Thank you for coming to sit next to me in my own home; what a beautiful red robe, King of the Universe. Lord, pour out your love here, I will scoop it up. I feel much better and feel at one even though I have no physical communion yet. I do indeed have you in my heart for sure. I gaze into the host circle – still don't know what that part of the apparatus is called – the circle that holds the host in the monstrance must have a name, the door that opens to it. The vocals from the chant music turned on inside the church are annoying; I prefer pure silence so I can hear your voice, Lord. Tonight the monstrance looks like gold hair, flaming out on all sides. I imagine the six candles are my three daughters and their future husbands.

Lord, do you want me to increase my quiet time or am I sufficiently paying attention? Lord, I pray you remove from me any addictions and afflictions keeping me from guarding the six lights in my life I feel charged to protect. I'll follow you, Lord, and they don't know it but by "tracking" Mom, they're following you without knowing. Just by association, it can be enough.

Starting classes tomorrow is like going back to my baptism at age 9 and getting to be raised all over again, but as Catholic.

August 21, 2025

The day has arrived. The journey is about to begin. It's the first day of the Order of Christian Initiation for Adults (OCIA). To mark the milestone, you won't believe what happened. I came across two rosaries I didn't know I had, belonging to my stepmother and my grandmother. On the same day I start OCIA, I found both rosaries, in two different places at two separate times, completely by accident. That's like seeing a double rainbow on a journey about to begin.

There are about 30 of us who enrolled in OCIA. We watched a video about the El Camino de Santiago, an historic pilgrimage route in Spain since the 9th century. We are about to be pinned with individual scallop shells after we all get turns introducing ourselves. Also known as "the way of Saint James," the 483-mile route leads to the cathedral in Santiago de Compostela where the remains of Jesus's disciple James are believed to be buried. The scallop being a long-time symbol of the Camino de Santiago, we too are on a pilgrimage at home of becoming Catholic.

As people talked, I wrote mine in my head in case I was next: I wasn't raised in the Catholic Church, but my Episcopalian grandmother insisted my brother and I be baptized when I was nine, Dec. 28, 1975. In the 1980s, I joined the Church of Religious Science (Ernest Holmes, not to be confused with Scientology), and then in the 1990s, joined Unity Church from Unity School of Christianity in Unity Village, Missouri. I relied solely on 12-step programs for another decade, until a 2013 born-again Christian salvation, making my way to Citizens Church when it opened its doors in January of 2014 in Redlands. After 10 years, I felt called to another church, but then was called again to the Catholic Church. *Should I talk about my experience where the Eucharist unveiled itself right before my eyes at The Holy Name of Jesus?*

Better just to listen to others. I have a long way to go, and feel I'm keeping faith a secret. On YouTube today, I looked up how to say the rosary, but when my daughters came home, I quickly turned it off. Is it shame or just a need for spiritual privacy? Hiding my faith is wrong; it's what caused me to not nurture them spiritually growing up *and I'm still doing it. This has to change.*

August 22, 2025

I dipped my newly found old rosaries in the church holy water then brought my rosaries to Father Thomas to bless them. I shared with him the story about discovering them in my home not even knowing I had them, on the very same day of starting OCIA classes. I wish I could have captured the words he said over them for their blessing. Sometimes these holy words go right over my head like my mind can't grasp the language, even though it's English.

To my surprise, he said he had a question to ask me after he blessed the rosaries. I reeled at the possibilities at what I could be doing visibly wrong from May 31 to August 22, so visible he would notice and feel the need to ask me a question. That's the other thing. I hate being noticed, *and yet I'm dying for attention.* Explain that contradiction.

He asked: "Why do you come daily but not take communion?" I told him I was only starting my OCIA classes that night, not Catholic yet. He said he wondered what could be going on in my spiritual life that I was not taking communion, so had assumed I was already Catholic.

Then I just had to blurt out: "Would Jesus have made people wait?" I instantly regretted saying that, especially because I didn't intend to ask it. He replied with kindness something about the nature of authority in the Catholic Church and wanting to make sure people are ready. He spoke about the ancient practice of forming and preparing people for full reception into the community – mutual discernment between the inquirer and the community being entered.

Just that a priest would be interested in what could possibly be going wrong in my life made me feel seen, heard, and counted. *Like here's a church that really cares about the state of people's souls.*

Food never tasted so good as it did today, tonight's dinner of wild rice, mixed steamed vegetables, and raw extra firm tofu just heated in a microwave. The hungrier I get spiritually, the more fed I feel by my healthy earthly food. Because now I can tell the difference between the two types of hunger. And yes, Satan worked overtime today trying to ruin my desire to write, whispering in its slithering serpent tone: "What if writing about it all makes a mockery out of you, the church and God?" I spit back mentally, "What if it doesn't?"

Yes, I do feel left out every day of the feast everyone else gets. Who among the eligible would choose to miss even one heavenly meal? It's not fair that those who don't receive communion have the ability but no passion, and I have the passion and no ability right now. But a recent homily came to mind about the immature nature of "it's not fair," so that put an end to my inner tantrum. It does feel like a punishment, however, like I'm being denied spiritual food. So, I have something to work on. I think it's called *patience,* and maybe even regard or respect for the ways and reasons. Still, I tallied up my lost meals from age nine. Multiply 50 (years) times 365 (days) since baptism, and my missed heavenly meals to my birthday May 18, 2025 amount to 18,250. No wonder I've felt spiritually starved my entire life.

It would be great to see a movie about one life in parallel – one version receiving the Eucharist, another version of the same life without it. I'll have a before and after story. The movie I don't want to see is ever going without it once I get to have it.

Another 330 heavenly meals are going to pass before my eyes before I can receive it officially. I've invited you all before, but I'm inviting you again to the Easter Vigil service at the Catholic Church nearest you. It's the Saturday evening before Easter Sunday, so April 4, 2026.

I have this unnatural fear of dying before I get to receive the Eucharist. The fear caused me to look up a potential loophole I haven't confirmed: Apparently, if I were in danger of death, I could ask for the Eucharist. I'll remember that if I land in a hospital before April 4, 2026.

The non-Eucharistic life I've discovered to be a sort of limbo state that's more like purgatory but on earth. I am neither Catholic, and no longer Protestant, but tracing back my religious history to baptism and bringing it forward.

What would happen if I told someone Jesus paid me a visit, but not only that, wearing a kingly robe? Or what if I told my girls or their dad that this happened? Why am I ashamed of my relationship with Jesus? I have tapped a well of shame I didn't even know was in me. I can totally see how someone entering the doors of the Catholic Church would confuse this inner well with "them," the Catholic Church. In other words, it's shame inside me, but I call "them" the shaming ones. Projection, I think it's called. It would be easier to blame the church and "them" for shaming me rather than admitting to my own shame. I could even blame them for exposing my shame rather than owning it as originating in my own life.

The Catholic faith shines light on all warts and dark spaces, so be forewarned. I'm not used to such a spiritual workout. Today it went to next level socially. As if last night's class wasn't hard enough, 30 people in a circle summing up how we got here. I attended morning prayer in the courtyard for the first time – the Liturgy of the Hours. Josette introduced me to what felt like a hundred people in my overwhelm, when maybe it was half a dozen. Last night I hadn't been able to say a word to an American-born Ukrainian woman, Oksana, sitting next to me, when I wanted desperately to express my concern for war in her homeland. "Going mute" was still pressed the next morning.

Not only do I lack the language for explaining Catholicism here, and at home with my daughters when they ask, "how was Mass?" I also can't find the words for what I'm experiencing, which is why I write two hours a day to grasp the words. It's like a full-time job becoming Catholic. *What if my enthusiasm burns out?* There goes Satan again, masquerading as my self-esteem, or lack of it. Speaking up in class is going to be a challenge for me not to over-do it or under-do it.

Staff members told their stories last night briefly, and I learned the term "cradle Catholic," born into the faith. I'm starting to think the *absence* of faith growing up is *spiritual abuse.* All my life, I've heard complaints from people raised in religions, while the rest of us just don't even know what we're missing.

Then at night I hopped on my first "Zoom Rosary," meaning a group from church gathers to say the rosary on Zoom. The rosary in my mind seemed like the Bach piece I started at age 12 on the piano and failed to learn fully. It seemed endless and complicated until this night, when we got through it all together as a group and my two sets of rosary beads were officially resurrected from the possession of the two deceased mother figures. One of the prayers we said at the end of our group session is called the Unity Prayer. It was *way too intimate for me.* Here are the words, see for yourself:

My adorable Jesus,

May our feet journey together.

May our hands gather in unity.

May our hearts beat in unison.

May our souls be in harmony.

May our thoughts be as one.

May our ears listen to the silence together.

May our glances profoundly penetrate each other.

May our lips pray together

To gain mercy from the Eternal Father.

I'm just not used to being so close to God. And I'm still not sure what is so objectionable to me about proximity, but it points to the source of lifelong intimacy problems with others. I now see that it's my intimacy problems with the Lord that caused my intimacy problems during marriage. Where I gave up on my marriage too early, I will not give up on my church. I will not let my intimacy issues chase me out the door. Here I will face all the spiritual intimacy issues with the Lord that I ran from while married, for the first time, without even being married to someone. I'll get to do what I failed to do when I was married. The church creates the same pressure cooker as the married life did for me, as a vessel. I'm called to be every bit of what God wants me to be, just without a husband.

This is a good time to give you a concrete example of how food can block intimacy, and how that relates to the Eucharist. I was married from 1992 to 2008. Both of us were baptized Christians, but I hid my love for Jesus behind his agnosticism. But that isn't the point I'm trying to make, just the context. Whenever I would binge, I wouldn't want sex. There was a direct link between eating sweets and then not wanting to be intimate.

The same is true for the Eucharist. Now that I've been sweet-free for five years, there will be a finer intimacy when I have communion with the Lord than I have ever known. To equate the Eucharist in sexual terms may seem less than holy, but what we eat directly influences our ability to become intimate. The enemy uses treats to lure our noses away from intimacy with the Lord. What we eat can also dull our senses and even dampen our desire for communion with the Lord like it did for me wanting my own husband.

I'm sure there are people who can eat a donut and still have sex and take communion keeping that donut at least an hour before Mass to respect the fasting requirement. *I'm addressing people like me who use food as a wedge. You know who you are if you relate to what I'm saying.* Not all people who eat sugar are addicts, and not all addicts are people who eat sugar. But if you want to test whether you are or not, try removing the wedge. If it won't budge, it's a wedge. Or just ask the Lord and he'll tell you if it's between you and him.

August 23, 2025

Adoration

God bless my cousin's marriage of 45 years today. In my short exposure to Catholicism, I am already thinking of other people more often and more thoughtfully.

Lord, I will not be shy about my love for writing that you gave me. I will publish this book and begin a ministry for people to write about their encounters with the Lord during adoration, anything about their Catholic journeys. If that's what you mean for me to do, Lord. In the presence of the consecrated host, the words come directly from the circle! Today I pray that the Eucharist calls all people with eating disorders to experience grace.

I'm learning to use my words better. Catholic words from Jeannette flow like honey. Her first email to me, with permission to share: "You are a joy and blessing to have in our prayer group. When your daughters see your constant joy, they will want the same. You are the perfect example to them; to follow your heart in things of heaven. Walking with Mother Mary will make it easier."

Jeannette assigned me my first service position with the church! I was assigned an hour from 11 a.m. to noon on First Friday's Adoration which occurs from 8 a.m. to 8 p.m. Jeannette told me to search for a guide called the Magnificat Adoration Companion. I'm called a guardian, and my hour post is to just make sure the church isn't empty during adoration. *But it's much more than that.*

I'm on day 12 of the book pilgrimage and today is about wisdom and Thomas Aquinas. Kelly writes: "The world is drowning in information and knowledge but starving for wisdom." Catholicism teaches you how to be humble and quiet to listen for wisdom. I'm always trying to stand out somehow, be unique, special and noticed. First. Lord, please make shaping my personality less excruciating. I cannot suffer this much shame and embarrassment over the smallest things in my encounters with other Catholics. Even when I'm quiet, Satan whispers, "You're being too quiet."

August 25, 2025

I notice that I am more delighted by people now. This is a conversion in and of itself. Today in church, I noticed children's love for their parents, something I've not really paid attention to before. I know the Lord is softening my heart.

When the priest said "God loves you" over me this time, I said thank you while he was saying it. This is me in general, always interrupting somebody. I'm kind of a skittish animal, deer in the headlights, afraid of being caught making the slightest mistake on this narrow road. This is narrow. It isn't the "rules" people fuss about making it narrow; it's the call to be better people.

If the church knew how much I was starving spiritually apart from the Eucharist, would it feed me like the poor on the street? The agony increases with each passing day and feels cruel and unusual with all the eligible people out there who let the Eucharist pass by day after day without care. *Can't I have theirs?* This reminds me of never getting picked for jury duty when I'm the only one in the room who wants to be chosen Something is going to have to shift in my deprivation mode, or I'll become resigned to indifference. Either I must stop looking at it as deprivation and start respecting the rules or self-combust in my own impatience. Something must give.

How does Jesus handle all the human rejection? Do we really want to increase his suffering by ignoring him at the altar after all the suffering he did for us on the cross? *He misses us* and wants to be with us through the Eucharist. Jesus has been missing me as much or more as I have missed him, and maybe even felt sad 50 years waiting for me to come to the table, so what's eight months on my end? Plus, I heard in the old days, formation in the Catholic Church took people three years.

This is the longing I was trying to fill with food and coffee until 2020. This is the pure longing I drowned in those substances. Now I feel it in the raw with no barrier or filter, so yes, the temptations to eat cookies and drink coffee are acute. But if I were to indulge in them, it would erode my desire for the Eucharist: I wouldn't notice the longing or feel the need. Instead, the desire will morph into looking like it's those binge foods and drinks I want.

Whatever foods or eating behaviors make us feel guilty – those are the signs it is a misplaced desire for the Eucharist. If it's excess, we consume food that could be used for other people. The goal is to not put that excess between me and the Lord. Heavenly food belongs to the Eucharist only. You can see it in the demeanor of the Catholics who look so appreciative, holy, devoted and devout, during communion. It's so beautiful to watch.

I've never wanted anything more in my entire life – this Eucharist. What will I do when the intense longing is no longer there, once I am able to receive it? Today I realized the truth of the Eucharist exists whether I partake or not, so this helped calm down my impatience, resting in the truth of the Eucharist itself. That it existed long before I was born and these last 50 years since baptism means that it was no less available to me then than it is now. Maybe my First Communion will shore up 50 years of neglect because it will be that powerful, like I was never apart from it.

August 26, 2025

Every day, I must witness the moment of transubstantiation in the Eucharist. I can't miss it now because I know what it is. I'm sorry, Lord, I haven't responded to your invitation until now. I'm late for supper. Having prided myself on being early to all things as a way of life, this is particularly humbling. As part of the 33-day pilgrimage book, I signed the historic petition to Consecrate America to the Eucharist; I'm #298,797 of the half-million milestone we're all aiming for, and someone named Yusuf Aminu was just before me on the website, consecrateamerica.com.

August 27, 2025

Watching TV, when I look across the couch at my three girls' profiles all in a row, I find such love for them. And I think, is this how God feels about me? If so, I want to respect that love so deeply that I wouldn't do anything to offend it. Everything I do has to reflect that love he has for me.

The goal of being a good person is worthy. Living from the love I have for Jesus is what permits me to be loving toward others. I'd like to write about noble things. My first book was a disappointment to my mother, and she would have abhorred the second one about sparing children from divorce. With this coming book, we may have been able to have our first spiritual conversation. After she died, I felt her love for me expanded somehow, as did mine for her.

August 28, 2025

Lord, to me it's scary to join a church where persecution and targeted hate are a focus. Two children died in Richfield, Minneapolis, yesterday when a shooter shot into the Mass at their church right after these words were repeated: "If I say 'surely the darkness shall hide me, and night shall be my light' – for you, darkness itself is not dark, and night shines as the day." And right before the alleluias about to come, the gunman shot right through the stained-glass window. They were just about to say: "Whoever keeps the word of Christ, the love of God is truly perfected in him." And all this was just 10 minutes into the Mass. The entire attendance was prevented from receiving the Body of Christ.

Our church is connected to a school, Sacred Heart Academy. They attend Mass in our church. Normally I would give in to fears and avoid Mass just hearing the news report, but instead I prayed harder and attended boldly, even with compassion for the troubled soul who did this. That's new, though I shouldn't be congratulating myself for feeling compassion. I'm at least feeling it on day 16, almost halfway through my 33 days to Eucharistic glory pilgrimage. Indeed, I am less afraid of the harsh things in the world as I feel new spiritual armor. And I feel purpose in my prayers.

August 29, 2025

There is a need inside for security that is beyond human failing. When we try to fit a person into that spot only meant for God, they cannot measure up and are doomed to inadequacy in our eyes.

Likewise, it's easier to feel rejected by a person than it is to admit to feeling the absence of God or admit the need for God. If we are feeling rejected by a partner, this could be a projection of our own rejection of the Lord. We need to look at the rejection we are doing of the one who created us and loves us most: Jesus. And put an end to our rejection of him. Then we feel less rejected by other people, if at all. And will probably do less rejecting of other people, and the Lord.

Becoming Catholic isn't just about acquiring knowledge, because one can always know more. It's about having a heart for God with a desire to be closer to him. It's always about clearing away what's between me and God to receive the Eucharist in a worthy manner, and what that means about my life as it is now, compared to what it needs to be.

Prayer has really taken the edge off my overeating urges and the feeling of being spiritually starved, also removed my focus on deprivation. While I'm waiting, why don't I stir up enthusiasm among my OCIA classmates? I told Oksana I hope my spiritual wildfire doesn't consume me or burn out so fast, like some 90-day wonder. She said she thinks the same spirit I feel now is exactly what will prevent burnout. She's right! This is not addict energy that easily crashes. I see the Lord's mercies are new every morning just like Lamentations 3:22-23 says. "The steadfast love of the Lord never ceases, his mercies never come to an end; they are new every morning; great is thy faithfulness." Not even renewed, but new altogether, as if for the first time. See the difference?

August 30, 2025

Day 18 in the book's 33-day pilgrimage discusses how the Eucharist helps with disordered desires, because of its benefits: Friendship with Jesus, the desire to know and do the will of God, cleansing of venial sin, hunger for virtue, grace to avoid future sin, a heart listening to Holy Spirit, desire to know and love God. I feel like I have all these benefits right now just by beholding the host every morning. This is precisely the application of the Eucharist I was looking for regarding eating disorders of all types.

My physiology changes during adoration. My mind feels sharpened, whether I entered feeling dull or not. Something solid gets added to my heart which fortifies, and the back of my head feels padded with light. And this time I felt fed by the Eucharist with my other senses – the sound of the music accompanying the gold around the circle, the light filling the space between me and the monstrance.

The Eucharist can give "the long view" of life. I'm thinking, what are you going to have written about you five years after your death by those who remember you? I want to be known for my joy in the Lord, enthusiasm, early rising, and writing. Lord, guide my pen! Maybe when people buy a new journal, they'll think of me writing to the Lord. That's enough. But what if I'm underestimating?

Daily Mass has added so much spiritual muscle to my life. After three months into it, I feel it's as much a part of my life as food, exercise and sleep. This is the time to wake up spiritually in the world, and this was clear watching the Pope be elected on May 8, 2025, online. So instead of falling into the political divide, I could instead rise with religion and transcend it, answer to a Higher Authority.

The Eucharist far surpasses any previous desire for Jesus, so the religious track record almost feels erased since age 9 baptism. The best is yet to come! And while I can appreciate my patchwork history for it leading me to this point, the present is where the real journey unfolds.

I don't have quick answers for my children, semi-curious about my conversion. One daughter asked me,

"Do you believe in the devil?" I answered yes, late at night, with explanations as to why. But I corrected my answer in the morning that I don't *believe* in the devil. I believe in Jesus, but I know the devil is to be reckoned with as an evil force. But I don't put my faith in that; I put my faith in Jesus. She understood the difference in semantics. I could have deeper answers; I grasp words that haven't formed in my mouth yet. For example, I neglected to ask her thoughts on the topic, or what even brought it up.

September 1, 2025

The Lord is removing all the non-essentials from my life – random half-commitments, new propositions for work or activity, unfinished projects that just needed closure, this seems to be a season about emptying, including the nest when my youngest daughter sets off to college next month.

Day twenty on the 33-day book pilgrimage is love. Today is my father's birthday in 1933. He died in 2019. Early in fatherhood, he left six children on the west coast while he fled 3,000 miles from his own guilt to live his own life. I equated "the father" with vacancy. Love = Absent. Knowing what the Eucharist has in store for me, this vacancy will soon be filled. The love of Jesus is greater than I can comprehend.

What I believe the Eucharist will do for me: I will feel spiritually fed. It will finally hit the spot I've been trying to fill with treats my entire life until five years ago. I will feel whole in my relationship with Jesus. I'll feel closer to other people. *There will be no more absence of the father, because I will abide in him.*

September 2, 2025

As I draw closer to the Eucharist, up comes the usual historic interferences. In my mind, I plan the perfect binge, but now I know the coffee cup is just a distortion of my desire for the sacred chalice containing the Blood of Christ.

How will I make it through the next seven months with all these food and drink cravings interfering? Carrot cake was perfect September food in 1981 to treat the trauma of our house burning down. So today in memory, I wanted the perfect cup of plain Starbucks coffee with milk, and a slice of carrot cake from Albertson's. The fact that this binge feels like a concrete plan is so disappointing. It deeply disturbs me knowing that once I indulge, I won't care about the Eucharist at all anymore. I just feel it in my bones. That's how marked a distraction it is for me. Satan whispers, "It's just one cup of coffee and one slice of cake," when he knows that that's all it takes to carve out my soul and usurp my union with the Lord. No, thank you.

All my life I was more devoted to coffee, ice cream, cookies and chocolate than to anything else. And my private worship could go unnoticed because I wasn't obese. No one could tell I worshiped these foods so acceptable in our society. I could even overeat and then blame *having to wait for the Eucharist until April* as the reason I picked up my binge foods, but they are really masking a desire for the real presence of the Lord. *I could get away with all this if I was unconscious of it.* My only recourse is to abstain and wait patiently for First Communion.

All this lifelong nonsense with food will vanish once I take my First Communion, I just know it. I've waited 50 years, what's seven more months of conscious waiting now that I know what I'm missing? A binge feels like it would be disgracing the Eucharist, not preparing me for it. I'm really seeking and wanting God when I seek to binge.

I just need to be redirected. The binge is a distortion of the need for the Eucharist. That's why binges are so empty – it's never about *that* food and its fleeting pleasure. *What I'm really after is the food provided only by Jesus in the Eucharist.*

September 3, 2025

I read an article in Catholic Exchange that sums up for me everything about the significance of the Eucharist, as well as why it's the most important meal I will ever have day to day. I wrote them asking if I could share it here and they said yes. It's from January 25, 2018:

https://catholicexchange.com/eucharist-food-journey/

What stands out most to me after reading the article is that *I'm enraged.* It's a miscarriage of justice that I have not known this truth until now. I feel betrayed without knowing against whom! "People in general keeping this from me!" I guess Catholics including Stephanie don't just go around passing out invites to the Last Supper. As the cravings for food and coffee try to step in as a cover-up, I know they are meant to mask the true spiritual craving I am now experiencing.

Satan's most subtle and original evil trick was and probably always will be around food, which is why it's the original sin. With food, all it takes is one bite to fall for the enemy's trap. Test it out. *You won't notice a thing at first. Then, silently and invisibly, it leads you away from the Lord.* So today the enemy uses whatever passes under our eyes, nose and mouth to lure us into the same fall from grace every day away from the Eucharist.

Come away from the table of gluttony, greed and excess that douse the flames of Eucharistic glory that could be burning inside of you. Choosing to abstain from the addictive and harmful earthly processed foods will naturally reveal the true craving of your soul for God himself. Stephanie calls her regular healthy eating habits to support the Eucharist, "God-honoring eating." I wonder why it took five years of abstinence from unhealthy foods and amounts for this true hunger to surface in me. I have survived so many temptations in five years. Was the divine hunger really buried *five years* deep under healthy eating?

Do not fear the deep spiritual hunger lurking in you. Walk into it raw and unarmed. Face it. Embrace it. It will not swallow you whole. However, I anticipate that communion might swallow me whole. I will be completely absorbed into the Body of Christ as I take him in. I will lose that sense that I am apart from God or anyone else. To this point in life, I truly only feel like I'm a separate entity, a leaf in the wind apart from the vine. But making the discovery that I am apart is what has helped hold me together.

September 4, 2025

Are more people converting to Catholicism? Yes! It's at a 20-year high in the United States, according to an AI search, with 160,000 conversions in 2025. Internationally it's up as well but can't tell how much. Perhaps people are called to deeper truths in times appearing to worsen.

Going to Mass daily and not taking communion gets me ready for receiving it. I'll be so ready for him, it will be like "instant Catholic, just add host." There's a lot that goes into the heart, mind and soul to prepare to receive the consecrated host. And there's a lot to be said for hearing the daily "Jesus loves you" from the priest every day in lieu of the host itself for now. So today because summer hiking is better earlier in the morning, I'll make the noon Mass in San Bernardino. *I won't miss the miracle of transubstantiation now that I know what's going on.*

I can't stand craving coffee. Today I envisioned walking into Starbucks and getting a cup. I prayed so hard at noon Mass to be fed by looking at the Eucharist and have the craving removed, even named it a demon and asked the Lord to cast it out. I saw the line of cars at Starbucks on my way to noon Mass and my past addict life flashed before me. Do I really want to get back in line after five years? I asked God to remove the longing. It's even interfering with my ability to write today, which is a two-hour commitment squandered in coffee daydreams. That's when you feel you must consume coffee just to relieve obsession. But then it takes over. I was off it for eleven years once, and then after having it again, couldn't be free of it for an entire decade. *Thank you, God, for my five years without coffee.*

September 5, 2025

First Friday Adoration

I must ask the priest about my guilt about writing during adoration. I read online that it's considered disrespectful to write during adoration. But I'm conflicted because I write to the Lord and best connect with him in writing. It's just that last time I did it I thought the woman next to me was glaring at me, or maybe she was just mad at her husband and happened to glance my way at the same time. Either way I took it as I was doing something wrong. I'll have to ask if it's ok.

Come look at your life through the lens of the monstrance holding the consecrated host. Stare into the eye of the needle. Come lose or discard whatever nonessentials are cluttering you. Come face your personal demons and watch them invisibly flee. Feast your eyes on the spiritual food Jesus said is ours. Come pick out your favorite stained-glass color in the church. Come behold the Creator of the Universe alive with us today. Come experience physical changes just sitting still: a boost in circulation, restful restoration, tingles at back of head, relaxed and regulated breathing, a softening face. Come dream deeply again at night after you leave here. Come to the table of heaven and earth.

At this adoration, I became aware that normal food feeds my body but doesn't touch my soul. I've never felt this separation before. I was always trying to feed my soul with food and drink. But I'm distinctly aware now of a space inside just meant for my soul's food. No wonder I never felt satisfied before! God revealed there is a difference between how my food is assimilated at just the level of the body, and how it will be assimilated when I take communion. There's no cross-over between the two types of food.

I wrote to my selected patron saint of writers for the first time: St. Francis de Sales. I got the feeling he didn't like my book's subtitle. I also felt him calling me to St. Francis de Sales Catholic Church in Riverside to write. I got the feeling I'm supposed to publish this in advance of the Easter Vigil. I get to name a patron Saint at First Communion, so I've chosen the patron saint of writers.

My dream life is undergoing major upheaval! I must be transforming at the deepest level. I've been prone to earthquake dreams my entire life, but this one was totalitarian in nature. Everything was spinning and compressing and everything "died" – except my consciousness didn't expire; I was aware I was still alive. Perfect peace.

Then another dream: Back to the first man I got engaged to only five months after the divorce finalized. In the dream, I was about to marry him, already dressed in the gown, until suddenly I told the first guest who arrived that *I can't choose a man over God and I can't have both.* Imagine that, hindsight with foreshadowing! How's that for soul confirmation I'm a consecrated woman?

Then another dream: Director Mel Gibson is at a table and I'm about to tell my story of becoming Catholic, but right when I think he'd be most interested in my Eucharistic epiphany, he sits at a table with the catechumens and ignores me. *I will no longer seek the attention of this world* is what this dream says to me. *I will give my attention to others.* Also, in our OCIA group, more excitement is truly deserved for the first-baptized! So, go Mel. Can't wait to see his sequel to *The Passion.*

September 6, 2025

I'm on the virtue of "awe" in Matthew Kelly's book "33 Days to Eucharistic Glory." I show up to Mass daily to not miss this miracle, when the elements become the body and blood of Christ. This being the case, do I really need to ask for an alternative wafer to reduce my body's reaction to wheat? How would I seek this option every day? Wouldn't it drive the priest and the line crazy, me having to ask for it every time? I still haven't resolved whether I need a low-gluten alternative.

Today at church there was a Jubilee event with the relic of St. Bernardine, and when I thought they said "it is her skin," it creeped me out. Why does everything Catholic have to be so...intimate? When I looked at the relic, I couldn't see what it was, maybe it was cloth, clothing or leather skin of something. A statue is coming to church next weekend, but not just any statue. Lady Fatima. Catholics really pray for others a lot, like non-stop. I must work on my intimacy issues to keep up the pace.

Inherently selfish, I keep to my family pod like a mama orca. It's difficult to embrace the church as a family. *But I have to grow in community.* I don't feel comfortable doing the rosary as one of the readers yet on our Friday night Zoom but will try to stretch myself next Friday. Getting to know people isn't going to be easy. All my life I've lived in a 12-step program bubble, except for my children's 22-year school community, so even my track record of leading people to Christ just includes one recovering alcoholic mother and one former fiancé who maybe just accepted Christ for me. I feel woefully inadequate about how to be useful in drawing people to the Lord, not even imparting it to my own family. It's like we had a no talk rule about religion growing up, and my mother instead overtalked politics. And then as a mother, I just carried on the same way, minus politics.

Everything about Catholicism promotes self-care of the physical body. I've suddenly added a hand weights routine to my exercise routine, started treating my dry skin with lotion without realizing how parched it was, and trimmed my nails better. When I drink water, I think of it as holy water I feel blessed by.

Tomorrow in Rome, Carlo Acutis will become the first millennial saint. I'm going to watch online in the wee hours of Pacific Time USA. *He said he didn't waste a minute of his life doing anything He knew God wouldn't be happy with.* I know God doesn't want me to worship Starbucks. I have my eye on trash in a field at the intersection of University and Central Avenue in Redlands, and next time I get a coffee craving, I'm going to use that addict energy to clean up that spot instead.

September 8, 2025

Today recognizes the nativity of Virgin Mary. My own mother was a Mary, died Sept. 12, 2022. My stepmother was Mary Ellen, died May 7, 2020. **I now claim Mother Mary as my spiritual mother**. Now I can pray to her about mothering, asking Mary to guard the hearts of my three daughters all the days of their lives. Each day is something special in the Catholic faith. My bare notes here day to day don't do it justice.

Today at Mass I felt deprived of the holy meal. I've only been used to feeling deprived of foods that are *not* good for me. The deprivation of sugary foods is a small sacrifice. Waiting on the Eucharist, which is good for me, feels like a huge sacrifice. But God is slowly shaping the way I view this deprivation until next April. I focus on the person receiving the Eucharist in front of me, as I bow. And I get as close to the sacrament as the priest lets me, with my arms crossed, as the priest says, "Jesus loves you."

Back to those physical changes I'm undergoing. Now that I've added food to my regular meals, I'm less hungry and more fortified to embrace what spiritual hunger comes until next spring. I feel more solid, sound, strong, and deeply peaceful as a person. And this is a good thing, because the last of my children goes off to college in about 10 days.

Last Saturday I went to the annual church kick-off. The people are so *nice.* I like the genuine sparkle in their eyes and voices. One woman told me she thinks "Jesus adores my smile." Who talks like that? Catholics! I've never once thought about how Jesus would react to me as a person. But these are the concrete ways of developing a more intimate relationship with him. Soon, I'll be a nicer person, too, with new words to write and speak.

Think about how the Lord sees you. It's love beyond what you feel for your own children. Ask him more questions. I ask him regularly, who is this book for, Lord? It's for the people who are missing the Eucharist *who are eligible to receive it.* It's only September and I have written a full journal already. In two weeks on the first Monday after college drop-off, I'll visit St. Francis de Sales in Riverside, where I felt called to spend time writing.

It's also not easy to generate the stamina and mental vigilance to keep on the same page every day as all Catholics on the liturgical calendar, a system I have yet to understand. But I feel ready for this newfound discipline and will return to the Liturgy of the Hours in the mornings after Mass when I have finished my last breakfasts with my youngest daughter at home under the roof of her childhood.

Catholics truly enjoy their religion. Look at all the people in Saint Peter's Square attending the canonization of the first millennial saint. Listen to the grounded joy in Pope Leo XIV's voice. See the delight in the face of a father who holds his baby up to be blessed by the Pope as he drives by in his Popemobile.

In my own church, I see the enthusiasm for the visiting relics of the saints in the Jubilee year. It's so festive. And I love how excited people get for me when they hear I'm becoming Catholic, because I don't know what's in store for me. There are a ton of books, pamphlets, magazines and online material to discern, podcasts and posts, and of course, the Catholic Bible. It can feel overwhelming, but when I return to focusing on the Eucharist, it all simplifies again. Daily Mass simplifies it all for me, integrates it into one, no matter how complicated it starts to feel.

September 9, 2025

My patron saint's quote is on the September calendar of prayers for each day today in the *Living with Christ* monthly magazine Stephanie sent me. St. Francis de Sales, patron saint of writers, wrote: "Divine Savior, we come to your sacred table to nourish ourselves, not with bread but with yourself, true bread of eternal life. Help us daily to make a good and perfect meal of this divine food. Let us be continually refreshed by the perfume of your kindness and goodness. May the Holy Spirit fill us with God's love." *My role model.*

My writing life is kind of a secret. I have a ritual where I pray before the Lord and then write two hours a day. I offer my writing talent to the Lord, ask the Holy Spirit to guide my pen. But I also looked online and found a lovely prayer in an article by Pam Spano dated August 15, 2015 at Catholic365.com: "May the Lord guide me and all those who write for a living. Through your prayers, St. Francis de Sales, I ask for your intercession as I attempt to bring the written word to the world. Let us pray that God takes me in the palm of his hand and inspires my creativity and inspires my success. St. Francis de Sales, you understand the dedication required in this profession. Pray for God to inspire and allow ideas to flow. In his name, let my words reflect my faith for others to read. Amen."

I can invent any new prayer in the day or pray naturally, spontaneously, for St. Francis de Sales to intervene, guide, understand, and inspire. But I also like the idea of praying for other writers who are trying to achieve the same goal.

Much to my delight, I discovered two things about my patron saint that relate to my life: His birth date is August 21, the date I began my formation classes, as well as an original long-term abstinence date from my food addiction.

His death date of December 28 is the date I was baptized on the calendar in 1975. As I become Catholic, he'll be with me here on out for my vocation as a writer.

September 10, 2025

During Mass today, I clearly heard the priest say, "Blessed are those called to the supper of the lamb," and realized that I am one of the called and therefore am blessed. This is how I got here; I asked the Lord if I should be taking communion, and the response was, "Come to the table." It's the strongest I've ever heard the Lord's voice.

At Mass today, I wanted to scoop the entire bowl of wafers into my mouth like the cookie monster from "Sesame Street." At least I'm craving the right thing now – the Body of Christ. Maybe it will help to surrender greed for Lent this year, or maybe I shouldn't wait that long to give it up. The desire for the entire bowl is probably because I view it as forbidden for now. Something about it harkens back to the Garden of Eden.

September 11, 2025

Becoming Catholic feels a little bit like joining a convent, because of the call to holiness and sainthood. Now that I reflect, I was only 7 years old when Julie Andrews starred as Maria the nun in "The Sound of Music." I liked how she was a great mother figure and religious but got the message that you choose a man or God but not both. I chose men from age 15 onward and made them all God. My twice divorced parents reinforced these ideas with their worship of partners and absence of God.

I wonder what my mother, father and stepmother think of me becoming Catholic. From my father, I would get a lecture on how Catholics aren't liberal enough. And my mother would object to my consecrated woman status.

My stepmother would be glad that her lifelong diatribe against the Catholic Church didn't keep me from discovering it.

Becoming Catholic is like a distillation process, a filtering process, taking out the impurities coloring my personality and tarnishing my heart. I've become softer, kinder, no edge to my tone, no anxiety in my pitch, no hastiness. Just ask my three daughters ages 18 to 27. They'll tell you: "She's chill."

Now I have a new reputation to uphold. But so far, I'm way too self-centered to call myself a real Catholic. I've done volunteer work my entire life, believe me, I know how to work for free. But this time it will require selfless giving of time and motives for God. There always had to be something in it for me in the past, no matter what the cause. This time it needs to be free of my own personal or professional ambitions, something I don't know about yet. I'll figure out where to start. Regarding money, I gladly give 10 percent of my income to the church. Beyond tithing, however, giving time and money will be a stretch for me.

Being Catholic makes it easier to handle tragic world events. Here's why: The regularity of Mass keeps the enemy from derailing your mental thought process. Every 24 hours we get another boost from the Holy Spirit. Being rooted in the spiritual food of the Eucharist, we are fortified against other temptations. I receive this fortification just by contemplating what it's doing for others, and what it will do for me.

Any suffering we must endure can be seen through the lens of how Jesus suffered for us. And we have hope where others might not. I can't speak for other religions, but this one church experience here makes me feel authentic for once and also like I found the true way to express my reverence and worship openly, socializing less to keep the focus on Jesus strongest.

This helps me face world news daily. For example: My heart feels heavy for this 9/11 on its 24th anniversary. My mother died three years ago tomorrow. Subway victim Iryna Zarutska stabbed to death for no reason after her pizza shift. Public assassination of Charlie Kirk conservative activist leaving behind two small children and a wife. Being Catholic makes me care where I didn't before. I was much more comfortable not caring because I didn't bother myself with anyone else's crosses or burdens to bear, and I certainly didn't help them bear them. I have complete faith that receiving the Eucharist will treat every ill, ailment and issue I bring before it, with some kind of physical or spiritual grace like I've never experienced before.

September 13, 2025

The ominous sound of an owl in the forelight starts my morning quiet time. Lord, I feel I'm being prepared for something special that only I can do. Please bless this unique mission, whatever it is. All you need is my faculties and wits about me and a strong body, and me and my three daughters will be protected by all the angels and saints. As I become more like you in my heart, Lord, I fear my demise. I feared death on my mom's death anniversary yesterday. I feared traveling to Long Beach for fun yesterday.

A new interaction with a man at the gas station shows me I'm changing. He asks me, "Need some help over there?" I reply, "With what?" My mind ran the gamut from needing earthquake straps on my bookshelves to removing excess dirt from the back yard to scanning for precancerous cells to have frozen off. He said: "What you're doing there." I was just getting gas. I replied that I could always use prayer. "You work at a hospital?" He noticed my red and white OCIA pin of a scallop. "No, I'm turning Catholic!" That locked me in: "Spare some change?" "Sure, just a minute." I lock myself in my car and find my $5 bill meant for this purpose. After I drove off, I realized for the first time, I didn't evaluate whether he deserved it or not. I felt the same about him, whether con man, drug addict, or simply needy. Mercy me!

Saturday Adoration:

The statue of Our Lady of Fatima is visiting our sanctuary for adoration. Instructions I received from the host during contemplation were clear: "Uncover every dark corner." The monstrance creates a lens to see your life through the eyes of God. Crying over my youngest daughter's halftime childhood, I pleaded in my heart for the remaining half back, and God showed me it was wholehearted mothering even if half-time custody. I've not been without her for a minute and never will be. *It was my misconception of "half-time childhood" that created my pain.*

Filter all things through the Eucharist. Bring all things to it. Let it consecrate your life. It will tell you the truth about your life. The Eucharist is wholeheartedly living in Jesus, in his body not just spirit, with light, grace and protection. And adoration of the Eucharistic host activates this.

Do we have funerals here? I'd better tell my kids. Lord of hosts, guardian angel, who are you? Visit me in a dream, please! Lord of hosts, write my book! Guide my pen, Holy Spirit. Create words in me to feed others, words like medicine. The Eucharist is like a tuning fork for alignment and re-alignment. The words drip onto the page like honey!

September 14, 2025

Sunday morning
Exaltation of the Holy Cross

It's my youngest daughter's last Sunday before going off to college. Her dying cat is still alive. Today ends my 33-day Eucharistic Glory pilgrimage. I need to read my "consecration to the Eucharist" prayer before the tabernacle. There will be no empty nest syndrome for me. Not only are both older daughters living at home, but I'm building a nest branch by branch, twig by twig, by becoming Catholic, a nest in my heart that is an eternal home for them to come home to.

September 15, 2025

I feel like I'm getting married next April 4, 2026. Then I read about why this is, during my 33-day book pilgrimage that ended last Sunday on the Feast of the Exaltation of the Holy Cross. I'm in spiritual communion with the Lord, but not yet a physical communion. I've never become one with the Body of Christ, both in the sense of God and Body of Christ referring to people in the church. This union is new. And maybe I've never known it, since my own marriage 1992 to 2008 didn't include this profound experience of God in the sacrament of marriage. I wonder what we will wear for the First Communion next April?

Yesterday I got to talk to the priest because after Mass I got in line like everyone else does who wants to say something to him. I wanted to share my conclusion of the 33-day solo journey and ask for a blessing. Father Thomas's words flowed over me like a waterfall, but I only remember the word "heart." Remembering that one word is enough. And bridging my fear by getting in "the line."

At that moment though, I felt greedy! I already have so many blessings, shouldn't I be asking him how I can go pour out blessings? The only place I have to pour right now is this diary.

Today at Mass I thought about how important the person in front of me is, when I get to bow behind them in line as they receive the Eucharist. I silently pray that they remain reconciled to the Lord and are made holy by the encounter. I receive my daily "Jesus loves you" from the priest in lieu of the Body of Christ for now, but I also feel the duty to be there for the person in front of me. This is new!

I'm imagining what I'll share at my first confession, because I'm so current in my work already in Step 10 of my 12-step programs in which "We continued to take personal inventory and when we were wrong, promptly admitted it." But I made a list. Want to hear it? I confess: That I failed to raise my daughters to know and love God. That I left my one and only Christian marriage. That I committed adultery multiple times in my life. That I cohabitated with men. That I worshipped food and coffee over the Lord. That's my short list so far. I could come up with more by April when I give my first confession to the priest before taking the Eucharist.

Why would I openly confess in a book what's privately meant for a priest? It will give me more courage to say it privately with a priest if I practice doing it here. I'm warming up. It's easy to admit to you in a book, much harder to take it before God. It will require more courage for me to go alone before God with a priest. I can't wait for that holy experience I've never had. Plus, it's easier to tell you my faults than to accept forgiveness for them.

September 16, 2025

Today at Mass, I realized that not partaking in communion while I wait to become officially Catholic is a lot like how I show up to family celebrations at restaurants. Everyone else eats, but I just enjoy the company eating my own food I brought with me. So today for the first time, I really felt I could settle into this mode of grateful acceptance and contentment for the remaining months. Enjoying the daily celebration without eating is something I'm used to, because even our meals at home I'm on a different schedule than the others, though our meals sometimes do coincide. I'll be eating lunch when they have breakfast, for example, and I'll just have water while they enjoy sushi at a restaurant on a Saturday afternoon.

The blessing for everyone at the end of Mass is more than sufficient, as well as the anticipation of the Eucharist. Luckily there isn't anything moral or behavioral I have to correct that I'm aware of. For example, I'm an unmarried woman but devoted to purity in my singlehood. There is no active sin in my life, not even the venial ones *that I know about.* That was a word I had to look up: venial. Right now I feel ready for communion, and my Catholic sponsor agreed. But there's an order to things in the church, and it feels protective, respectful, and loyal to the OCIA group to follow it.

September 17, 2025

I can be with the Lord at home in my morning quiet time in the wee hours, as I've done for decades now, but when I sit in church during adoration or Mass, and before, it's the "Our Father" with his people I encounter. This is a huge difference.

The difference is God "in the world" vs. just at home with me. It's like I felt the Lord most with me in the moments before open heart surgery in 2019, but magnified times ten, because it's God in his totality, for everyone, the entire world. And at church I get to be with him and *everyone else.*

And as I link up with *everyone else,* my life comes into a fuller perspective. This morning, I realized that when I was 19 with my mom in Paris, at 4:30 a.m. we visited the steps of the Basilique du Sacre Coeur de Montmartre so mom could paint the sunrise. That's the same place, the Basilica of the Sacred Heart, where the adoration has been perpetual for 140 years! To read about it now and piece it together with my own "pilgrimage" there in the past, well, it just shows you how you can be blind to anything right in front of you. I just thought of it as a pretty church mom wanted to paint. The end of insignificance, forty years later, just by having the memory fall into the modern context of becoming Catholic.

This inspired me to try something new: Before I napped today, I asked for a dream or vision like a hungry person would want to be fed. And I dreamt of "the dewfall" phrase from the Eucharistic wording! I am so serious, it's the first dream-on-demand I've ever had. If I were an artist, I would paint it. But words will have to do:

Deep red flowers in a small garden bed. The petals on the flowers were Jesus's blood. Clear tears dripped down from the flower petals into the soil. It was the most beautiful red I've ever seen, and they were not known flowers. It's as though they were tears of grace dripping from the petals, and they were watering the soil. I woke up like my soul had just been drenched in the dewfall.

The condition of my soul had revealed itself to me in this dream. Perhaps it's because my favorite line during

Mass is the moment before transubstantiation when the priest prays for the Holy Spirit to descend like "the dewfall" to transubstantiate bread and wine: "Make holy, therefore, these gifts, we pray, by sending down your Spirit upon them like the dewfall, so that they may become for us the Body and Blood of our Lord Jesus Christ."

I never felt so nourished by a nap in all my life when I woke up just 10 minutes later. I wonder if this nourishment is what it feels like when you receive communion. Perhaps this is just a taste of what's to come.

September 18, 2025

The Eucharist defines the point where Heaven and earth touch. It's even more of a secret kept from people who don't know Jesus yet. But to those who know Jesus already: If someone told you there's a place on earth you can go every day to experience Heaven on earth, wouldn't you want to go? That's what it's like just watching the consecration of the host – the liminal space is like a portal where Jesus shares himself daily all over the world to Catholics partaking in the Eucharist. This is the best kept secret on earth. If you aren't holding your breath at that moment already, it takes it.

In my deepest soul, I never would have imagined being Catholic and what it could do with me, for me and to me, and what it will eventually help do for others around me. It was something "those people did." Not sure why at 59 I'd find it while others were born into it. But I see God's design, and the work he has for me ahead. The paths people are on differ so greatly, but so many weave their way into and out of this faith, and all paths emanated from this faith in the very beginning of Christianity. I already sense the Holy Spirit working through me more, using me, guiding me, shepherding me throughout the day. It just requires constant vigilance, alertness, watchfulness, and wakefulness.

Today I heard back from Paris! I made an inquiry about the 140-year perpetual adoration at the Catholic Church in Paris, where guests can stay overnight in the Basilica Guesthouse to participate. Here's what Sister Renee Marie had to say: "It was the Basilica of the Sacred Heart of Montmartre that celebrated the 140th anniversary of perpetual adoration this year (August 1, 1885). Every evening, we welcome guests to lead worship services between 11 p.m. and 7 a.m. Guests are accommodated at the guesthouse and commit to worshipping the Lord for one hour each night by signing up on a designated board upon arrival. At 9 p.m, an introduction to the night of worship is offered." Here's a link to find out more:

https://www.sacre-coeur-montmartre.com/messes-et-prieres/adoration-perpetuelle/ladoration-perpetuelle/

Isn't that so beautiful? I wish I had the painting in the collection of world watercolors my mother left behind. That means someone else has it somewhere in the world, with a little Mary Moore signature in the lower right corner. Sometimes she just signed her work MM. It means we were there on the 100th anniversary and didn't understand that Jesus was inside, waiting for my memory to return in 40 years.

September 19, 2025

Trying to determine if my urge to do life without a car is a monastic desire, a premonition to save my life, a St. Francis "give up your possessions" move, or Satanic sabotage. It feels like God's will to walk everywhere possible. Walk the earth. Driving just does not feel holy or safe to me anymore. I had another car crash dream that felt prophetic. Dreams evolved from near misses to actual crashes, as if because I wasn't responding, the threat was increasing. Once sold, the peace descended like the dewfall. I had finally heeded the warning and can now move on to another topic. I look forward to saving money, meeting people, getting more exercise, and preserving lives by staying on the sidewalk.

We put down my youngest daughter's cat today, with us for 16 of her 18 years. I secretly read the cat's last rites, looking online for them. I'm no priest, nor do I know if last rites apply to animals, but I said them aloud over her privately anyway. My little cat-alic. I'm glad she lived to see me turning Catholic. I read online that merciful euthanasia is ok for animals in Catholicism, but not for humans – cautionary key words about animals, "read online." We made the decision in a family group conscience.

Some people don't like "the rules" they call the Catholic teachings, but I'm more fascinated by learning the reasons behind them, their historical intent, and following them. For example, CCC 2324: "Intentional euthanasia, whatever its forms or motives, is murder. It is gravely contrary to the dignity of the human person and to the respect due to the living God, his Creator."

No rule is going to chase me away from the rightful relationship I deserve with our Lord. These rules are meant for the integrity of this relationship between me and Jesus. I'm tired of finding out the hard way that we are punished by our sins, not for them. It took gluttony to stop eating sugar, for example, which is why I eat well now. It's easy to tell if something is a sin because *it punishes.*

September 20, 2025

At Mass today, I attended on a full stomach for the first time, forgetting the recommended hour of fasting beforehand. I saw how when you go on an empty stomach, Mass is a different experience. I noticed I didn't feel connected to the host by looking at it, whereas my eyes otherwise feast on it. This occurred even though I wasn't consuming the host. I made up my own one-liner for those of us who can't partake yet: *Feast your eyes on him with holy hunger.* But keep to the one-hour fast guideline for practice.

Maybe I put food between me and the Eucharist because I'm emotional over my last daughter going off to college today. If I wasn't so happy for her, it would be easier to notice my sorrow about her leaving childhood behind. I'm just glad that as I turn Catholic, I'm noticing that I put other people's feelings before mine automatically now. What a relief to become less self-centered. It was the core problem in my previous book.

Social media in general freaks me out, but I took a risk and posted in our church community on the Hallow app for the first time at 5:50 a.m. I asked for prayer from our community "for all the college freshmen moving into dorms, including my daughter." Stephanie told me yesterday we Catholics don't do anything alone, so my last daughter going off to college is a community affair now. My plan is to keep trusting the Lord and Mother Mary with my daughter's care. When I checked later, 67 people prayed for my daughter! I realized that if I were to hide out in a faith community, I would be keeping prayers from her.

September 21, 2025

Mass at St. Francis de Sales Catholic Church
Riverside, California

As soon as I saw the baby's breath bunches at the altar, I knew why the Holy Spirit pointed me to a nearby town to visit the church. I had just dropped my youngest daughter off at college, and the baby's breath at my wedding had foreshadowed her existence fifteen years before she arrived. It was such a special touch to my soul that the baby's breath is now on the other side of that, heralding a new journey for her and for me. Who uses *just* baby's breath? Usually it's an accompaniment flower. It was too coincidental to not be noted as *just for us.*

Then when I went up for the communion line, the priest recited words over me in Latin, so I have no clue how special they were, except for the exponential holiness of Latin. Then a man who obviously isn't Catholic *knelt* while arms crossed over his chest, me thinking how come I didn't think of kneeling? Could I do that, too? Kneel during my own turn in line even though not receiving the Eucharist yet? Again, another moment of spiritual shame of source unknown. I feel so unworthy of asking these detailed Catholic questions.

Then at night, I responded to an invitation to attend the "Choral Vespers for the Jubilee of Justice" at Our Lady of the Rosary Cathedral in San Bernardino. I liked going to something with no clue of what it would be, but simply because Father Erik invited the church community there. I learned how to stay on my knees for the longest time ever during the silent prayer time in front of the blessed sacrament. Such spiritual exercise caused me to sweat beads down my back even though I wasn't hot, strengthening the muscles in my knees, and feeling my circulation swirling, knowing it had to be a good thing. I've never prayed with my whole body before until this moment, which seemed like 30 minutes after so many glorious songs, yes including some in Latin. The harmonious interaction between ours and other local churches really is new for me and such a wonderful community exchange. The group photo at the end became a snapshot in life I would have missed had I been shy, claiming to not know what it was about. Every day is a chance for something new.

September 22, 2025

For example...I finally got up enough courage to ask Father Thomas today after Mass if it's ok that I write during adoration. He affirmed it was quite alright, part of the contemplative experience. This simple lesson teaches me to think of what I'm thinking about when I look at other people. Am I seeing them, or my own thoughts?

On this first day of fall, I've followed the lead to walk to and from church, and it energized my entire day. I'm selling my car just to operate without one for a while, to be more still, and to turn exercise into transportation, but mostly because I was guided to sell it. Everything about driving looks greedy to me right now. Drivers look way worse from a pedestrian view than they do driving among them. I discovered the four-way stop intersection near my house where *no one stops.*

Another historical suspicion arose toward the Catholic Church again after I applied to work at the Native American, the Yuhaaviatam of the San Manuel Nation. Satan whispered, "You can't join the Catholic Church because they abused the Native Americans converting them." *Nothing is going to keep me from my relationship with God.* Any aspect of history can't come between me and the Lord. In other words, it would be dishonest of me to allow anyone else's human behavior to keep me from my right and real relationship with God.

September 23, 2025

I'm becoming familiar with saints. Padre Pio made an impression on me today, official name St. Pius of Pietrelcina. Today is his day. Three important things I read online to do on his day: Confess sins, make a voluntary sacrifice, and pray the rosary. Apparently, the enemy gets agitated on this day with all the spiritual stirrings. And one of the great mysteries of Catholicism I've discovered is that there's no standing still, even though it's all about how to be still before the Lord. The contradiction is rejuvenating and mysterious. I'd already decided to sacrifice my car, and I needed to confess to Stephanie that I was eating breakfast before taking time with the Lord upon awakening, intending to use food as a buffer between me and God again. I truly want to see God first, not the kitchen. And my intention with the rosary this morning was to repair generational sin. "Mother Mary, please enter my house! Break the curses of my lineage on both sides of the family."

Ever since I started keeping this diary it really makes me think about what's most important in the day. No matter the state of the world, we can walk forward boldly with confidence that our heavenly existence lies ahead. There is no fear of death, but of course that's why I'm selling my car tonight, since driving is the most dangerous thing I do. Owning a car felt greedy and excessive for my station in life right now.

September 24, 2025

First official day without a car, and it's a new life. While I now pose a pedestrian risk to cars, or riding with someone else as a passenger, I have eliminated myself as being the cause of any accidents and significantly reduced the possibility I will be involved in a collision. I cannot explain the liberation of this "sacrifice" I made on the day honoring Padre Pio that asks us to sacrifice *something* in the name of leaning into the Lord. It takes 50 minutes to walk to church. On the way there, mini graces include smiling at a Jack-in-the-Box worker just getting off her graveyard shift and observing how many people still smoke while driving solo with open windows. Turning from University onto Citrus Avenue, I inhaled a block-long wall of jasmine I grew up with in La Jolla. Once I got to Mass today, I said my Spiritual Communion Prayer from page 144 of Matthew Kelly's *33 Days to Eucharistic Glory*:

Jesus,

I believe that You are truly present

In the Most Holy Sacrament of the Eucharist.

Every day I long for more of You.

I love You above all things, and I desire to receive You into my soul.

Since I cannot receive You sacramentally at this moment,

I invite you to come and dwell in my heart.

May this spiritual communion increase my desire for the Eucharist.

You are the healer of my soul.

Take the blindness from my eyes,

The deafness from my ears,

The darkness from my mind,

And the hardness from my heart.

Fill me with the grace, wisdom, and courage to do Your will in all things.

My Lord and My God, draw me close to You, nearer than ever before.

Amen.

Two seconds into kneeling in the pew, up comes the deep fear that someone is going to ask me to do something I'm not ready for, capable of, or able to do, rooted in my premature exposure to sexuality. Naturally, I offered the fear up to Jesus with my thanks for removing it.

Conversion is physical. There are going to be more physical changes ahead and maybe I need to eat more food now that I'll be walking so much. That is, until the new church is built only half a mile from my house. I could get a bike, but I'm loving being on foot and walking feels safer on blood thinners for a metallic heart valve. Lots of life between my home and church that I was whizzing past daily. As I walk past the high school, it gives me a chance to pray for the students and parents I see at the morning drop off.

For a moment, I wanted to start a *sell your car* viral campaign. Sell your car and see how it changes your life overnight! Remove yourself from the freeway rat race. Slow down and let life bloom around you, on foot. Not everyone can afford this luxury of giving up the car, *but what if you could?*

September 25, 2025

Walking to Mass is a daily adventure, now part of my Catholic journey to connect with people on the streets. Walking past the high school, I saw two happy exchanges between parents and children as they were dropped off. A truck load of tree trimmers smiled at me so I smiled back.

Or maybe my smile caused theirs. On the way home from Mass, I examined the bus schedule to plan for tonight's ride home from OCIA. Unable to really figure out a single ride ticket on my phone, I just decided to walk. So many people from church offer rides, but I don't want my choice to go without a car to become their burden. Or I'm just too shy, or selfish, to let others help me.

I joined the group that says the morning prayers known as the Liturgy of the Hours after Mass. Today the words were so powerful as I focused on articulating. I've been a reader but not a leader yet. I use this app I Breviary for readings and it contains things we don't end up using sometimes so I wouldn't know what to skip. You can't have a fear of doing it wrong, becoming Catholic. You just have to go with it until God removes your fears of being perfect.

Earlier in the morning, before Mass, is my Quiet Time with the Lord. Many things happen in that time, but one of them is not eating breakfast beforehand. He is the first greeting of the morning now, not my oat bran, yogurt, milk and fruit. Somehow even my healthy meal snuck in there as a wedge between me and the Lord. Like someone who insists on their cup of coffee before reading the Bible. But now I have it in the right order. This morning was exciting because I was guided to recite the Hail Mary in Latin, being that using the Hallow app is so helpful to follow along.

Issue of the day: Being Catholic will help me forgive past perpetrators in the Catholic way. There might have to be quite a few amends redone with my newfound Catholic lens, to forgive with any fullness I lacked previously.

Back to Latin. The English language isn't as beautiful as Latin, so I gave myself my first written lesson in how to pray the rosary in Latin. Latin is the most beautiful language I have ever heard, and I only last heard it in grade school when we learned a bit of it. Try saying it, without even knowing what it means, then I'll give you the English words:

Ave Maria, gratia plena, Dominus tecum. Benedicta tu in mulieribus, et benedictus fructus ventris tui, Iesus. Sancta Maria, Mater Dei, Ora pro nobis peccatoribus, nunc, et in hora mortis nostrae. Amen

Hail Mary, full of grace, the Lord is with thee. Blessed are you among women and blessed is the fruit of thy womb Jesus. Holy Mary, mother of God, pray for us sinners, now and at the hour of our death. Amen

Walking everywhere is so liberating from time and space. My cardiologist will be proud of me when I meet with her in January, as she was trying to bump me up from 30 minutes a day cardio to more. That surgery in 2019 to fix a heart murmur from birth was profound right beforehand when the chaplain prayed over me. I felt the hands of Jesus cup my heart from within my body, under my heart! *My sister didn't know this, and when she arrived to take care of me for two weeks, she brought a necklace of the Lord's hands holding a heart.*

Today the physical response to Mass was breathtaking, literally. I lost my air right about the time he ended the Mass with a blessing, after which my air returned. Even my breathing patterns are changing, from someone who holds breath to someone becoming more calm and solid, with slower speech and slower breathing. All the walking is undoing years of confined driving and forcing the slowing down of schedules.

Assimilating all that is Catholic can feel overwhelming. Each day, the message of the homily can shift your world view in one phrase, so listen carefully. Here they teach you how to listen to the voice of God. I never had that at any other church, where sometimes you could be looked at funny if you said God told you something. Here it's just par for the course, and no need to be ashamed to share what the Lord is speaking to your heart. So even though I get uncomfortable on a regular basis now, it's because I've never grown so much since I began the conversion process.

I did declare to my Catholic sponsor Stephanie yesterday that I am a "consecrated" woman. It's not on the list of "single, divorced, married or separated" on medical paperwork, but it comes closest to single. One definition is this: "Set aside to live as a bride of Jesus. She will never marry a man; instead she gives her heart entirely to God and lives a life of prayer and service for him alone." That is so me now. Any and all dating and seeking relationships for me ended in October 2021 when God seemed to sweep up my sexuality, heal it from past interactions, and set me on new footing with him. Even the reason I seek annulment after becoming Catholic isn't so I can be free to marry someone else, but rather to become right before the sacrament of marriage in the church. Annulment for me is more like an amendment to the Catholic sacrament of marriage, to set the record straight. It's acknowledging that my initial commitment was lacking in its understanding of sacramental marriage from the start.

Like I said before, no one tells you how much fun this religion is! It's like they wait for you to see for yourself before they celebrate with you that you, too, find it joyous. No one Catholic has ever proselytized to me, not even Stephanie, but in my previous churches, someone was always imparting their viewpoints unsolicited or talking negatively about other religions. *Here, I just don't hear criticisms of other faiths.*

What's the *fun* in Catholicism, you ask? There are so many choices of ways to honor the Lord and serve him. There are so many ways to practice the faith in all areas of our lives. It feels like a spiritual playground where I've been let into the building that reaches up to the gates of Heaven. And they open each morning through the portal of the Eucharist where Jesus comes to share his real presence with us, to partake of him, and really live and dwell in our very bodies right now here on earth. And when you start looking at your life through the kaleidoscope of the Catholic Church, every day of normal existence just becomes a mysterious adventure. An ordinary chore, sitting down to hug my adult child and having a chat, fixing a meal, taking care of business tasks, is all elevated to some new station in life I can't really explain. Yet.

At OCIA class tonight on the topic of Adam and the fall into original sin, I picked up on what it looks like to say "No" to God: Addictions, avoiding people, not praying, not communicating, not following God's will, living in sin. And what it means to say "Yes" to God: Live in truth, follow his will, abstain from addictions and sin, practice disciplines, love people, feed on his word, keeping in contact with the faith community.

September 26, 2025

On the way to church this morning at our Friday location, I got to say hi to children in pairs walking to school, I saw a church setting up for a yard sale, and I saw the morning swim workout of the University of Redlands team. The college clock tower stood like a morning sentinel. Ferocious dogs defended their owners from behind feeble fences, so I got my taser ready in case one jumped over on me. And I see I have the same problem texting while walking as I did texting at stoplights while driving. I looked up the name for "fear of driving" and it's "vehophobia." None of the options to treat it included just not driving. I think I've discovered the perfect solution to vehophobia, if I have it: Walking.

Attending Mass for the Blessed Sacrament of the Eucharist is the daily rehearsal for the Lord's Supper come April. I say my Spiritual Communion Prayer right when I get there. So many people I know are Catholic but never said anything about their faith: a city official I know, a piano teacher, a member of my 12-step program. Now whenever I bring up turning Catholic in daily conversation, there's a person who was raised Catholic or is Catholic or was Catholic. Out in the desert I even ran into a woman whose childhood parish is mine in Redlands. I asked her yesterday why so many people resent being raised Catholic. She told me her church, now my church, saved her life as a child. And that she thought about switching religions to be with someone she loved, but just could not do it. But she doesn't go to church today. "Too much dogma." That's a word I don't know well. The dictionary defines it as "a set of principles laid down by an authority as incontrovertibly true." Nothing has bit me yet. Through the lens of daily Mass, each day feels like an eternity, its own life, start to finish. A whole entire life in one day. Not sure how this overlay gets placed upon 24 hours, but daily Mass changes everything.

When I attend my Friday church group on Zoom to recite the Rosary together, it's like I'm exercising prayer muscles I didn't know I had. The warmth of the people and their routine devotion is so comforting, and their kindness so contagious, I'm just a better person for it. Not to mention all the beautiful words that flow through my circulation now, because as I say them out loud, they invigorate my blood, I can feel it.

But nothing delights me more than the moment every day the priest beckons the dewfall: "Make holy, therefore, these gifts, we pray, by sending down your Spirit upon them like the dewfall, so that they may become for us the Body and Blood of our Lord Jesus Christ."

September 27, 2025

Saturday Adoration

At Mass today, two words stood out most to me from Father Erik's homily: "Pay attention." I paid attention to: "Never underestimate the transformative power of God's love." He also recited a now-favorite Psalm 107:9: "For he satisfies him who is thirsty, and the hungry he fills with good things." *That's my God!*

From the third pew, the stained glass from the back window above the church entrance reflects onto the marble base at the front altar. So fascinating to see that it looks embedded into the marble as if inside it. As adoration began after Mass, this image turned into truth about me: I'm now seeing through the marble of my existence. All the marble will crack and break and all that will be left is the purity of the stained-glass window. This is me becoming Catholic, the deep blue in the glass mirroring my spiritual essence.

Then I noticed the real white flowers under Mother Mary reflecting onto the side of the marble base. These represent the gifts I have to give other people in my Catholicism. I'm so thirsty right now, but I don't want to break the sacred silent merger between Mass and adoration. What's the incense for? The stained-glass image contains a crescent moon and Jesus holding the world. I like to think our world is cared for as well as our position in the universe. He knows our position, our condition, and we are part of his plan. We don't need our own plans; we need our roles within his plan.

Adoration is a physical experience. Both ears felt a very slow vibration, as if the host acted like a tuning fork on them. My eyes felt brightened by the gold of the monstrance containing the host. My breathing – like someone had opened a window in my chest. Meaning from my dream of the red flowers was further revealed – the "tears" dripping from the flowers were drops of the dewfall, the flowers somehow *were* the blood of Jesus and the grace dripped in clear tears from them. It was raining from the flower petals into the soil. This dream still feeds me every time I think of it, it was that impactful. Each recurring earthquake dream I have is breaking apart the marble encasement around my heart.

Being in the presence of the Lord is a beautiful experience in and of itself. The Eucharist invites simplicity, totality, generosity of time, the unwinding of thoughts, memories and dreams, expansion of the mind and heart, and relaxation in the body. It draws forth the darkest places of my being to shed light on their value, worth, truth or expendability. Today I offered up four burdens I don't want to carry any longer. What the host will do with them, I don't know. I probably can be more intentional, I just don't know how yet. In Catholicism, I aim. But most of this becoming Catholic has been about showing up and going with the flow, being so welcomed here. Just this morning on the way in, someone handed me a little book for free: *My Imitation of Christ* by Thomas a Kempis. In this simple gesture, I felt recognized for my passion for daily Mass and my potential for sainthood.

Adoration is prophetic in nature! I had a vision of a future grandchild, and a message from stepmother Mary Ellen to connect with her sister and niece in North Carolina. I've been writing to them. I really could interact with people so much more than I do. One ugly fact among all the blessings is that by becoming Catholic, *I'm realizing just how selfish I am.* Turning Catholic is turning your insides out for all to see, especially me. There's no escaping "the mirror."

By the end of the hour, I'd managed to forget I was hungry or thirsty. But I did go fill up at the water station before walking home. I'm going to miss the church interior green decor of Ordinary Time once the colors change at Advent. All summer long it's been supporting my growth, the colors helping nourish the new growth, hence the flower dream. I didn't want to leave. Lord, thank you for my blessings this past week, seeing my daughter off to college, selling my car, all provisions from you, and my good health.

Bedtime prayer: Lord, will you personally feed me the Eucharist in a dream, please? I'll take it from your hand. The hand I dreamt of several months back.

September 29, 2025

What a profound dream. My disembodied soul was carried into the entrance of the walled Old City of Jerusalem, and the feeling was as if "I have arrived!" What does it mean? It's so far beyond conscious understanding. It's been so long since I had epic dreams, so I know that the Catholic faith has engaged my soul 100 percent. I didn't even know there was an Old City until I looked it up online after the dream.

Lord, I long to be fed by the Eucharist. Is there any way in a dream, I could take communion with you?

October 1, 2025

On my biological mother Mary's birthday today, I said a rosary in Latin in her memory with the help of the Hallow app narrator. As I approached the fifth strand, I kid you not but *her* single tear fell down my right cheek. I could tell it was not my own, but from my biological mother, Mary. This reminds me of the day my father died in 2019. He died at 1 p.m. but had fallen into the death zone at 7 p.m. the night before. The morning of his death, he woke me out of a sound sleep: "Pamela, it's so beautiful, don't worry about a thing." I missed him by one hour landing on the Denver airport tarmac, but he had already "seen" what he needed to report. Just his style, as a former newspaper reporter.

Every day is a big day in the Catholic Church, so even "Ordinary Time" on the liturgical calendar is extraordinary. Today is the day belonging to St. Therese of Lisieux, aka little flower of Jesus, a French Carmelite nun by the name of Francoise-Marie Therese Martin. She wrote *Story of a Soul* and stood for "utter simplicity and profound trust in Divine Providence." I walked from church to the El Carmelo Roman Catholic Retreat in Redlands, a landmark I never visited though living here 22 years. I saw a member of our parish who introduced me to Father Gerald. So comfortable with priests now, I probably too loudly said, "Hi, I'm Pamela, new to the Catholic faith." "Welcome!" he said with amazement. No deep questions required or asked. Did I think it would be the Spanish Inquisition?

The chapel at El Carmelo is heavenly with the view of our local San Bernardino mountain range. If God doesn't speak to you here, there's much less chance in the outside world. Look up. Look around. Become as still as possible in your heart. Then breathe. *Breathe through your heart.* See the little blue flowers in the tiles at my feet? I wrote a prayer for my mother in the open book of prayers in the chapel, about her art left behind: "For the memory of my mother on her birthdate in 1930, may the flowers she painted rain upon her and her watercolors seep into the souls of all who behold her paintings when they find their intended homes."

I have a humble, innocent, childlike heart, pure and lit up with enthusiasm. Lean into the light, the depth, the breath. Lean into your careful steps and words. Be available as your children need you. Bless this time on foot. Pray we all become like little children in our hearts and words. A playful heart brings joy to the world. One sacred heart feeds the masses.

October 2, 2025

Insights are being lost as rapidly as they come. I can't retain them long enough to write them down. It makes so much sense why Thomas Aquinas stopped writing after one of his encounters with the Eucharist. Writers think they can capture experiences like photographers, but if the words aren't strung together the moment they occur, it can vanish. When you realize words act this way, it's like having to write two hours to come up with two precise words.

Today's memorial is for the holy guardian angels. These are the ones we were assigned at birth. That means my daughters have them, too, just like each had their own cat growing up. And apparently, I can send my guardian angel out on missions to intercede.

Then out of the blue, my oldest daughter brought me white roses, not knowing that it was her late grandmother's birthday just yesterday. She knows white roses are my favorite and felt it was time I had flowers.

Today I thought more highly of my role as the earthly mother of these three daughters, empowered all along with guardian angels unrecognized in my ignorance. *Thank you, angels.*

October 3, 2025

First Friday Adoration

I hear the refrain at Mass quite frequently, "If you hear the voice of God today, don't let your hearts harden." My heart hardened from fear over the years. I distanced myself from God for fear of what would become of me. Saints met a martyr's death, developed an illness, or died for another person. I have to shake the idea that if I become holier, and if I become closer to God, I will suffer more.

The only three people I would die for are my daughters. I've had enough suffering in this life. It's what caused me to ideate suicide in the first book. So I guess I'm not willing to suffer for the Lord as He did for me. Nor am I willing to lay down my life for another except in those three cases. Is this what a hard heart is? Shall I list my sufferings to see if they qualify as enough for this life? I listed them separately, then decided not to enter them in this diary. I gave them to Jesus. Nothing compares to what Jesus endured. Maybe that's the point.

With physical adversity, it's hard not to feel maxed out on my capacity after open heart surgery and being overtime on the heart and lung machine. You'd think I'd be more brave as a result, but the opposite happened to me. The wimp factor is huge now over the slightest thing. Maybe it's why I stay so healthy, to avoid the slightest physical ailment ever again. The Lord has saved me from the suffering I manufactured myself in my life, after the early trauma suffered at the hands of others that wasn't my fault. I believe I would trust more if I knew more about the purpose of suffering.

Soften the words out of my mouth, Lord. Form the words on my paper. Make them worthy of your love for me. Help me find words to articulate my love for you.

This morning during adoration, we recited together the Nine Offices of the Most Sacred Heart of Jesus and Immaculate Heart of Mary from the book, *Alliance of the Two Hearts*. In the office of the promoter: "May everything we do think of and say even our silence speak of our love for the sacred heart of our Lord."

How beautiful the intentions are in this faith. The focus on the pure heart hits the spot. Today I felt I got a heart transplant just reading through the nine offices. My stone-cold heart of childhood fears from just yesterday felt transformed into a soft one, pulsing with vibrant red.

Pay attention to interior life; it's a different life compared to what goes on in our comings and goings every day. It has a life of its own that runs outer life. Just putting the books away afterward felt like a holy task.

I thought this hardened heart issue would take months to resolve, and instead it took the touch of prayer in an instant. Since class last night to this morning, a heart encased in fear that was cold and hard from fears in youth, became bookended by the two hearts of Jesus and Mary.

Dear Lord, I apologize that I didn't know the condition of my heart was caused by fears of you, distrust, and faulty thinking. I feel I can trust being spared from self-manufactured trials now. That means I'll have the wits and capacity to endure what comes my way as long as I'm not generating trouble myself out of sin and ignorance of God.

October 4, 2025

What happens to sexuality once celibate?

Society teaches that we must meet our sexual needs, seek partners, and not be alone. It was news to me four years ago that the greater need in me was for God to heal that place. Celibacy as a state of grace recaptured the innocence and the purity taken from me as a toddler and restored me to the chastity I could have experienced before marriage. It also redeems the commitment to being faithful that I failed to keep while married. It's all around a healing state for me, given all the abuse and misuse of my sexuality throughout my childhood and adulthood until four years ago.

Freed of lust, sexuality is transformed from an addictive process and rendered into a state of grace bringing sacredness to everything about being alive. There isn't longing or craving, deprivation or repression, but rather beauty in being alive and enjoying all the other senses previously dominated by sexuality alone. Such physical holiness is enough.

Solitary singlehood without the responsibilities of dating or seeking, also enabled me to face marital issues I ran from, intimacy issues with Jesus, and define myself as a consecrated woman. We consecrated women just mirror the relationship between God and his church like married men and women do in their marriage.

Saturday Adoration –

People love just sitting in the presence of God. I notice their peace and ease in addition to my own and see them transform over the hour as well. I'm not as good at detecting any turmoil or stress in a person, unless they're crying, but I am a peace detector. The interior life when neglected makes the exterior life feel empty. Turning

Catholic is like turning your insides out and then letting the interior life be the main life, making the exterior life an expression of it.

Church meeting

In my first meeting to find out more about the Consecration to Jesus through Mary ministry at church, Father Hau said: "Prayer comes from the heart, but extends to the hand." Prayer and action go together. This is ever so clear in the Catholic Church. Helping others is a wide-open terrain I've yet to cross, but conversion to Catholicism seems to be the first requirement.

October 5, 2025

A dream I had recently came back to me. A giant serpent chasing me had already consumed an entire body before me, and I was next, though I wouldn't be able to fit until the other person had been digested. Then in the dream I realized it was my old self in the serpent! Horror! The serpent was chasing me, but had already devoured me, which means the new me is free of the serpent. It cannot devour me because it already has the old me and cannot even touch the new me. *This dream revealed to me my separation from sin!*

October 6, 2025

Joining the Consecration to Jesus through Mary group is giving me mom vibes I don't want to face. This is me projecting my own mother Mary and stepmother Mary Ellen onto Jesus's mother Mary, even more so with the same names. I wouldn't want to consecrate myself to a projection of either of them. So, I have to tread carefully here to make sure I'm consecrating myself to the true Virgin Mary and not a distortion. I think I'll save this consecration for next year's ceremony. I just got over dad being Jesus.

I've been attending Mass since May 31, but only just now realized that when we first start every Mass, the priest leads us through a group confession of sins. How have I been coming this long and not noticed the purpose of the opening?

The peace in the sanctuary after everyone takes communions is worth speaking about; there's a sense of spiritual satiation. I so look forward to this moment of fortification. I'm making room for this moment by practicing now. This is why I go up in line every day, to solidify the routine for the coming sacrament.

For three days after Mass this week, we have a visiting lecturer from the mobile phone app called Hallow. We're discussing unity with God, ourselves and others, and exploring how God wants total intimacy with us. Even the root word for adoration comes from "mouth-to-mouth," says our guide, Maddy Cole. I can handle such intimate talk better now that I've resolved some abuse issues, even though I haven't gotten to the mother ones yet.

Today in Maddy's session we practiced Lectio Divina, a formal way to pray, read scripture, meditate upon it, and contemplate. In this 15-minute exercise, I first expressed my intention to trust Jesus more. After discovering in OCIA that I held a deeply rooted lie, "if you get close to God, bad things will happen to you," we read the Scripture of the parable of the prodigal son from Luke 15: 11-32.

What leapt out at me is that it was *hunger* that drove the son back to the father. In the contemplative portion, I felt the Lord speaking to me: "If you could only see how trustworthy I am." To which I responded in writing: "Lord, I get it that your plans are not to harm me, that you have protected me thus far, so I trust you will be with me in any situation and not allow me to harm myself in any way." *This includes hurting myself with food before I have a chance for the Eucharist to treat me.*

October 7, 2025

Today is the memorial of Our Lady of the Rosary. I walked half an hour to church from the point my daughter dropped me off to turn onto the freeway to go to work. I said the rosary silently all the way in my head, matching my words to my footsteps. Today's intention: praying healing into sorrow of the Gaza violence from two years ago and since that date.

We bring all things before Mary through the Rosary. I have a mental pathway for it now, as if it's just been dormant. It's extremely powerful. Praying now is my most effective response to life. I am constantly praying for something or someone. I was three minutes late to Mass, not sure why my pace was slower than usual. I'm also starting to remember people's names at church.

How do you know if you put food before God? Ask him and he will let you know what and which foods and when! The Lord came to me in a vision more than five years ago wanting my coffee cup. Until this recent kingly appearance on the couch, this vision was the last time I remember being conscious of a visit from the Lord. In the vision, he came with both hands outstretched, wanting my coffee cup in one hand and my other hand in the other.

If the Lord came to you with outstretched hands, would you comply? I kept drinking coffee for another year. Then we came to a standoff on the balcony one night: I flat out told the Lord: "I'm drinking coffee until I die, and if you want me abstinent, you'll have to do it yourself." I went to bed, woke up in the morning to "Call Susan," someone I hadn't spoken to in a few years. She was still in my phone as a contact. The first thing she said was, "I have 10 months abstinent!" I followed her lead and that was the end of coffee.

Would you give up coffee if the Lord directly asked you to? It took me a year. Jesus was trying to remove the wedges between us. He surely is a hound of heaven as they say, chasing after us with his love and what's good for us, even when we refuse to cooperate.

I'm reminded of how many times I "came to the table" in my life for meals. In our house growing up, there was once a dinner bell that called us from the bedrooms to the kitchen. For breakfast, spinach omelets. For lunch, tuna sandwiches. For dinner, it was spaghetti or chicken. In the last five years, I've had four meals a day, so it's easy to calculate 1,460 meals a year over five years, 7,300 God-honoring meals. Compare this to the Eucharist, zero right now, but in five years, that equates to 1,825 missed Heavenly meals just by passing on taking the Eucharist daily. After April 4, 2026, at First Communion, I won't miss coming to the table.

October 8, 2025

Turning Catholic is full of holy interactions.

This morning, Father Thomas blessed the "Miraculous Medal" that Stephanie sent me, on it a vision of the Virgin Mary that appeared to St. Catherine Laboure. On another morning, Father Thomas settled my brewing guilt over not raising my girls Catholic by explaining exactly how sin differs from that. "Go in peace" he said to my mother's heart, dissolving my imaginary burden as though evaporating into thin air.

We practiced "imaginative prayer" next with Hallow presenter Maddy Cole. I contemplated Scripture where

Mary visits Elizabeth after the angel first visits Mary, and this is where I find this message about my own mother.

Mother Mary, will you visit me? I hear her gently saying, “First be reconciled to your own mother. Your heart is hardened toward your mother.” I ask her if she can help me with my own heart. Mary, can I give you my mother’s pain to make a grace of it? She informs me: In my own mothering will be my grace. This is imaginative prayer, putting myself in the scene of Scripture. And what a lovely thought, that grace will show up in how I mother my daughters.

In the Hallow app class, a fellow parishioner reassured me that the non-stop activity I find in the Catholic Church is really training for eternity, so “endurance training.” I feed on Psalm 107:9, “...the hungry he fills with good things.”

October 9, 2025

I must hurry up and get right with my mother before being consecrated to Jesus through Mary in December. The urgency of resolving this is that I risk transferring distrust to Mother Mary if I don’t separate my mother out first. I'll have to tell the ladies already in the ministry “No” to this year’s consecration. There’s no way to make this fear of transference sound sensible, but gone are the days, for example, of proceeding with a commitment without understanding it fully. I did this with marriage, and I don’t want to make commitment mistakes with anything else. OCIA is enough for now. The authenticity in the Catholic faith won’t even let you proceed beyond your capacity. *There’s no pretense in front of God.*

At our third meeting of the parish ministry this week with the Hallow app speaker Maddy Cole, I told my “unveiling of the Eucharist” story to a parishioner who told me the gift I received was *the gift of faith.* It seemed more like knowledge than faith. You can believe it's the Eucharist, or you can know that it is. I know that it is, so I don't just believe it to be. To me it isn't a question of whether it is or not, anymore. Is this faith, or is this knowledge? I think the gift that Satan would steal is my knowledge of the Eucharist, not simply my faith in it.

Then at OCIA class tonight, I learned that I'm already part of the Body of Christ because I was baptized. I didn't really understand my first baptism at age 9, but the Catholic Church is bringing it into context.

Interesting questions posed in class tonight: Is my life a tabernacle where God dwells? What does it mean for me to carry God's presence into my home, school, friendships? I wrote this down from the lecture: *God's presence fills the tabernacle so his people could carry him wherever they went.* It makes more sense to me now: God makes his very body available to all of us in the Eucharist, so we literally walk around with God in our systems wherever we go. And we can experience such nourishment every 24 hours just by going to daily Mass.

October 10, 2025

Reflecting on last night's OCIA class, I wondered, since Old Testament *kings and prophets* in the Bible failed with covenants, what makes me think I can keep the new covenant known as the Eucharist today? And no wonder, then, I feel I'm going to do something wrong at every turn. It's in my genetic composition passed down from the beginning. My life failures just fall in line behind theirs, taking my place among humanity's lot. But this is also where it all starts to make sense: Through the Eucharist, the new covenant the Lord makes with us *every day* is an eternal one I can keep, though no king or prophet.

October 11, 2025

A relic of St. Francis of Assisi visited our church today. When I touched my rosary to it, it occurred to me I'm in the company of saints. *We are all saints,* potentially. My 12-step recovery program just meant we weren't perfect, but we're still meant to become like saints and be like Jesus. Somehow this potential was lost on me, until now. It's okay to want to be a saint, even desirable. Why not? False pride, a good topic for confession, is *not aspiring to holiness.*

The Eucharist is both a sacrifice and a meal of thanksgiving. It's a sacrifice of his body and blood that we receive, and it's a meal that brings us closer to God to nourish us spiritually. It isn't a symbol for his presence; *it's his actual presence* brought down from Heaven when the priest blesses the elements.

Catholic thinking is new to me, because as a young adult in my own Christian searching, I subscribed to the belief Jesus was already within me. In that case, why the need to take Jesus from the outside to enter my body? My over-reliance and over-consumption on food pointed to needing some type of nourishment I wasn't getting. And with this "Jesus is within" philosophy, it's less of a relationship "to" Jesus or "with" Jesus, since he's within.

It took some undoing to externalize the need for the Eucharist as that being the only way to physically enter the Lord's presence fully here on earth. John Chapter 6 in the Bible helped me figure it out. But in relationship with him, and with him in the union of the Eucharist, I can see now how that's as close as a person can get to the Lord while on earth.

October 13, 2025

I guess I should admit to the deep feeling that something is quite physically wrong with me. I have such hope and excitement for what's going to occur after April 4, 2026, but what if life cruelly takes me beforehand? It won't be a car accident because I sold my car, so I've reduced my chances of that significantly. In these last few months, I've also had a premonition that I'm not going to be living much longer. But what if by turning Catholic, I'm just dying to the old me, and that's why it feels time is running out?

Either way, dead or alive, you can't look at this world as a Catholic and be anything but hopeful no matter how much worse it gets in the world. Because: 1. The Bible clearly shows things get worse before they get better. And 2. The Lord promises peace and life with him now through the Eucharist.

What more precious gift could I seek or want on earth or in heaven than to be one with the creator, and every day, in this manner? I feel ready to stand before the Lord if it were to happen today, my demise. I could receive the Eucharist on my death bed! And my girls would give me a Catholic funeral Mass, but only if I convey to them my wishes. How would they know otherwise? I'm going to have to start speaking up in my remaining time on earth.

October 14, 2025

Dear Jesus, fill me with dreams and visions to write about!

Another dream I had this past spring just came back to me. I dreamt an image of the hand of God. There was no story in the dream. Pieces of my soul are coming together as if the Lord is putting together a new puzzle.

It's like he's making a stained-glass window out of me and only he knows the full picture. But it's being assembled to what he truly sees me as, to accomplish his goals.

October 15, 2025

I didn't realize I'd encounter so many *mother issues* joining the Catholic Church, especially since my mother died three years ago. How is it that I project all my mom hangups onto Jesus's mother, Mary? Just because they have the same name? I guess it's just like I projected my father issues onto Jesus and priests, it makes sense the Virgin Mary would get all my mother Mary projections. Even though I decided to delay the consecration ceremony, I still need to resolve these pressing mother issues.

It was the blessed Virgin Mary herself who revealed to me that my heart was still hardened toward my own mother Mary. The touch of awareness from that one Friday adoration spelled out changes needed. There's only so much I can do with healing the body, apart from the Eucharist.

October 16, 2025

Today I realize I'm not friendly enough to be a saint. And to be friendly just so I can qualify for sainthood, isn't a genuine or good motive. This realization was defining for me rather than disappointing. I'm too silent, reserved, and introverted for the role. I could decide to try to become nicer, but that would require me going against my introvert nature, which I value more than kindness.

October 17, 2025

Today the remains of Saint Therese (Leseuiux) visit the El Carmelo retreat in town, but I feel scared away by the crowds expected, rather than excited by such a rare event. I won't pretend fears don't guide my decisions.

What's breaking down is all pretenses. So, I'm not pretending to be friendly, formal, fearless. This process is good for me, because it's causing me to get down to my core problems as a human being – a cold, selfish heart that needs to break open and be revived.

Seeing how I really am with people is bothersome. I care, but not enough to fully engage in their lives. I could go this way for years, just showing up to be around people but never quite involved. I lived this way for 10 years at the other church. I have a feeling the Catholic Church won't let me get away with staying the same, but I'm a little more concerned that it will be up to me to change, and what if I won't?

October 18, 2025

As a Catholic, Stephanie belongs to the Third Order seculars of St. Mary's of the Portiuncula Franciscan fraternity, and it has a three-year formation period. The intricacies of the Catholic Church are endless and fascinating. I could get lost in the maze if it wasn't all based on the Catechism, where same-page Catholicism is rooted.

Eucharistic Adoration was so satisfying after Mass this morning. Using the handbook in the pew, I paid attention for the first time to the song we sing in Latin as the incense rises at the altar, what translates to English as: "O victim bringing saving grace who open wide the gate of heav'n, Our foes assail and press us hard, give us your strength, bring us your aid" and more. The Eucharist is like an anchor for my heart, a compass for my mind, and a calibrator for my soul. Anything derailed comes back into alignment, almost like a spiritual chiropractic appointment where the Eucharist is the backbone of the faith.

Beautiful and unexpected things occur during adoration, like the feeling of holding all three daughters' hearts in my own. It came like a body memory of all their heartbeats once in my womb, only remnants are still there somehow. I feel love for them through the sacred heart of Jesus somehow. I wish I could do this with all people, but I'm not there yet.

It's also meaningful to be moved to tears and not have it be over emotional pain for once. These tears of grace flow mostly during my favorite Catholic sacrament of Adoration. How could something so simple be so compelling? The Eucharist exposes, like an x-ray, the condition of my most authentic self. It's a different experience every time I go, giving new meaning to the phrase "a living God."

October 20, 2025

I don't write these diary entries on Sundays. The pen rests! I might write to Jesus, but that's part of my private quiet time, not "work." Today I learned I'm a "contemplative." Definition: A person who practices contemplation. Contemplation: a) concentration on spiritual things as a form of private devotion, and b) a state of mystical awareness of God's being.

Being contemplative feels like a holy order. Stephanie calls me a contemplative and believes my writing has great potential. Now the "fortune cookie" on my computer screen looks even more possible in the context of contemplation: "You will reach the highest possible point in your business or profession." If my vocation is to be a contemplative, the high point of that for me, every day, is actually on the clock – it is getting up at 3 a.m., sometimes

2 a.m. *That is the pinnacle.* It happens naturally. It happens daily. It's why I love writing so much. My alarm clock is my heart and it goes off at those times.

It also shuts down after 6 p.m. at night. I had to explain to bewildering prayer sisters today why I can't join a 7 p.m. book study. It's so hard to be oneself. It's much easier to comply with what others ask of you, but much more stressful if you go against the Holy Spirit. It's better to define yourself by informing others how you are, rather than having them define you.

You can't fake it in Catholicism, because it will just show. I think it's why people come here and fear making mistakes. Yes, everything is visible, even if I wear my veil off center. Everything in Catholicism is intentionally intentional, including *who you are.* If someone had said, "Join the Catholic Church, you'll really be your authentic self," I would have laughed! My misunderstanding was that they *make you a certain way,* not that it would bring out the holiness in me in my daily life.

Becoming Catholic is about becoming more of who God made me to be. This didn't occur for me in previous churches or religious settings. From April this year when I published a book, thinking that was the goal, to seeing now that it's all about me contemplating the most famous man who ever lived, is a drastic conversion in itself. *I still don't understand why Jesus had to die such a brutal death, like the worst possible of all ways to die. And I really don't look forward to understanding.*

Stephanie said that starting on the first day of Advent, she and I are going to study a new book, and this one is called *30 Day Eucharistic Revival: A Retreat with St. Peter Julian Eymard* by Donald H. Calloway.

Sponsors in OCIA have interesting criteria. These are Catholics who can vouch for your journey. They must be:

A formally initiated Catholic, at least 18, attending Mass and holy days regularly, participating in the sacraments regularly, and promising to help the candidate live in accordance with the teachings of the Catholic Church through support, encouragement and prayer. Christians in OCIA that are already baptized and called candidates have sponsors. The people who are becoming Christians for the first time being baptized and called catechumens, and they name godparents. It's all starting to sink in. The formality is glorious.

In all the sincerity and reverence, prepare yourself for joyful outbursts even in the midst of Mass. When Father Ismael takes to the podium at Mass and quotes, "You fool!" If it didn't bounce you out of your pew, nothing would shake you out of your sleep state. I guess you had to be there. But the Scripture today explains it, Luke 12:13-21: "...God said to him, 'You fool, this night your life will be demanded of you; and the things you have prepared, to whom will they belong?'

My friend Karen Gordon in Utah sent me a text the other day in a response to my fear that I would die a brutal death if I turned Catholic:

"News flash - 100% of us die - and as the Apostle Paul said...to live is Christ and to die is gain."

Her truthful humor put an end to my fear in a flash. It also helped me reframe the death wish in my first book from suicidal ideation into divine understanding of truth.

October 21, 2025

Never have I been surrounded by so many people who openly love God and are unafraid to show it and share how the Holy Spirit has worked in their lives and the lives of family members. And never have I been so aware that today's Mass could be my last, and that every day that could be true until one day it is true. In morning liturgy, we pray for all the souls of people who are going to die that day. But I'm finally okay with mortality! I used to try to hurry death up just to feel in control of life, by self-destructive eating behaviors in my case. Now that I know I can live in Christ on earth through the Eucharist, there is no need to fear death, beat death, or cause death, because he died for us and overcame death. *And he gave us new life already!*

I used to have a callous ear, listening to people's ailments every Sunday morning a few churches ago when we passed the microphone on prayer requests. It made for a depressing Sunday morning. But that's how a hard heart responds to others' suffering – indifferent, distant, detached, depressed.

How did it get that way? Mother Mary revealed to me that my heart hardened because of how I responded to my own mother —constant fear. Mother Mary showed me what my heart is supposed to look like; I saw it in adoration. She showed me I still have too much pain in my heart regarding my own mother, to make room for other people.

Dreams I've had in the past are now becoming relevant to me. The dream from 2018: I was at church dressed like a bride, but there was no groom, and I started spinning like a tornado, rising in front of congregants. *This is becoming Catholic!*

At the time of the dream, I knew nothing about how Jesus is the groom and the church is his bride. With that failed engagement, I was too busy learning that remarriage is adultery.

October 22, 2025

When I wake in the wee hours, any time after midnight, I get flooded with great lines to include that dissipate in the light of day. They're like dreams you forget if you don't write them down right away. It's not like they return, either. They have one pass and I miss them. I can only hope to catch the next wave.

Today I watched the 2015 movie, "Spotlight" again, so I could see it from my new Catholic lens. In short, it's about The Boston Globe's investigative "Spotlight" team which won the 2003 Pulitzer Prize for Public Service for the longtime coverup of systemic child sex abuse by the Roman Catholic Archdiocese of Boston. In the film, the statistic says 6 percent of priests molest, but I looked it up and today's statistic is 4 percent.

Child abuse is not "a Catholic thing." The largest segment of people who abuse children are still parents. I looked it up: 77 percent of perpetrators of abuse are parents of victims, with 81.5 percent of child fatalities involving at least one parent.

To understand that Jesus also died for abusive priests, abusive parents, my own father, really drives home that no one is exempt from sin or mercy over it. To leave a faith because of past abuse in it lets the abuser also take the faith.

I wrote a letter to the molester babysitter and forgave him for abusing me and the other child, even though this pedophile died a long time ago. I meant the forgiveness from the level of Jesus who would forgive his sins, so it was different from previous attempts. Becoming Catholic takes forgiveness to a new depth.

Since the issue is too deep to contemplate for long, I'm back to obsessing over the wheat wafer, and whether I'll have a biological response even though it is transubstantiated. The scary online warning: "Some research suggests that certain carbohydrates can trigger the release of feel-good chemicals like dopamine, potentially leading to overconsumption."

I guess I'll find out next April whether receiving communion makes me want to go buy a box of Triscuits or a dozen donuts at 3 o'clock that day. Some unleavened bread products are more than just the wheat, too, they'll have additives like sugar or preservatives that affect appetite regulation and consumption habits.

According to Catholic teaching on transubstantiation: The bread and its underlying reality changes into the Body of Christ, while the physical properties and appearance of the bread, including its chemical composition, remain the same. So in a sense, the wheat is transformed into something new, and its substance is no longer just wheat. The physical properties and appearance of bread remain, but their underlying reality is changed.

In Catholic theology, the substance of the Body and Blood of Christ refers to the underlying reality or essence of Christ's presence in the Eucharist. This is what's known as a mystery of faith in the Catholic religion, which is why it can be hard to understand because it's beyond human comprehension. But that one day when I knew it was the Body of Christ for the first time; there was just an understanding embedded in me that only occasionally wavers into doubt due to the enemy's efforts to keep me from experiencing the Eucharist. The Catholic teaching is that it's the Real Presence, that Jesus Christ is truly, really and substantially present in the Eucharist, body, blood, soul and divinity. It's a beautiful mystery to contemplate.

Becoming Catholic is like awakening brain cells and neural pathways in the brain that have been dormant since my birth. It feels like anciently coded spiritual DNA. It awakens as I find the language to interpret my own experience.

October 23, 2025

Today for the first time, I led the group in the morning liturgical prayer! I said yes when asked before my nervousness had a chance to respond. I love our morning group, sometimes as many as 20 people, but the liturgy of the hours is so much more profound than I'm yet able to understand. All I know is, afterward, I feel turbo-charged on the most heavenly words in our English language.

Class was great tonight in OCIA, and I don't think I'll be able to sleep for a while or put it into words for you yet. Father Thomas explained how the church is really the bride of Christ. I raised my hand and said, "Is this why I feel I'm getting married next April? He confirmed that I'm *supposed to feel like I'm getting married next April* as we join the Catholic faith.

The wedding imagery is so attractive to me. It's like I get to participate in the holiest of all matrimonies even though I screwed up my one and only human marriage. Because I didn't feel anywhere near this holy approaching the marital altar then. And I didn't understand how marriage was a covenant, not just a contract. A contract is an exchange of services, but a covenant is an exchange of persons – one for the other. I never gave myself to anyone fully and now I can give myself to Christ fully through becoming Catholic. I get to experience the greatest covenant of all time made by Jesus Christ himself when he instructed us at the Last Supper.

And the church is also where we share with others what we have been given, so we as the embodiment of the church "are" the church for others when we are out in the community. Our testimony is in the way we live. I was so excited after class, I ran all the way to the bus stop. And then wrote way past 9 p.m. which is unheard of in my circadian rhythm. The Catholic definition of the church is visible and spiritual: (CCC 771) "The one mediator, Christ, established and ever sustains here on earth his holy Church, the community of faith, hope, and charity, as a visible organization through which he communicates truth and grace to all men."

October 24, 2025

I woke up at 2:30 a.m. knowing why Jesus came to visit me on the couch that day. He knew I would write about it and tell you. He didn't visit me because I am special! He visited me because he gave me this love of writing, knowing I would write about him. All three of the books I published so far include Jesus in one way or another, but in this, Jesus shows up in full color.

He's the hound of heaven, I tell you — Jesus. The lengths he must go for me to write about him; I wish he didn't have to work so hard to get me to talk. I haven't even told Stephanie yet that *Jesus visited me that day.* I told one friend I knew would feel validated by it, because we were swapping "Jesus visitation" stories, but I didn't even tell my own sister, and we tend to share everything. I shared it here in this diary. *Why am I keeping this secret from Stephanie?*

I don't get the feeling Jesus experiences unrequited love the way we would if we hounded someone we loved with such persistence. While we'd get arrested for stalking, or at least be issued a restraining order, Jesus instead just keeps appearing. And one day his appearance will be so obvious to everyone that we will all fall to our knees. There will be no ignoring him then.

All my life I heard from random strangers, "Jesus loves you." Now I hear it from Father Thomas when in the communion line and it's my turn. But what does it mean to love Jesus? The Catholic Church is showing me how and why to love Jesus. They're showing me he is my one and only.

A man about my age stopped his car at the bus stop where I was waiting and said, "Can I have your number?" I said, "I'm not on the market." He said, "You married?" I said, "To Jesus." I really just should have said I was engaged, because we aren't married yet. I'm promised to him already. He said, "Can I give you my number?" *What did he just not hear?* I wasn't scared, because I carry a taser and already used it to scare away a dog lunging at me. I wonder if I should get a car soon. But when I said "No" with a kind smile, he just hung his head like a rejected schoolboy and left. It was good practice acknowledging my betrothed.

I'm not saying people who date *don't* love Jesus. I was merely demonstrating that in my case, this response is the truth about my situation, and I said it aloud for the first time in a situation. As I said to you before, the Catholic Church still considers me in a marital covenant with the only husband I had from 1992 to 2008. I've chosen an unmarried state not because I prefer to be lonely or have issues, but because that's the way I am able to put God first.

Where's my engagement ring? I hope my conviction got the man thinking about himself. You wouldn't want to think getting married to an actual person makes you less available to the Lord. And you wouldn't want to make the mistake I made of making your spouse your God because you don't have God.

October 25, 2025

Humility is the topic of 4:30 p.m. Mass this Saturday afternoon. Father Erik saying pride blocks the flow of God's grace. "It is easier to manage the holiness of others than to face our own conversion." We are called to be transformed, by looking inward and fixing our eyes on Christ. And, "This week, when you catch yourself judging, say to yourself, 'God, be merciful to me, a sinner.' Let the Lord turn comparison into compassion." He quoted Mother Teresa: "If you judge people, you have no time to love them."

On the way to church, I picked up the first bag of trash today after looking at it for a month of walks just passing. I had my bag, goggles, mask and gloves to avoid contamination. This is my field work, clearing up ignored public spaces a bag at a time. When you walk, you see the trash of the world. When you drive, you only see the trash in your own car.

I once worshipped alcohol and then worshipped food. But after quitting drinking at age 22, the food got worse. I worshipped Hershey bars my entire adult life until I first quit in 1991. It truly is possible to make food a god and put it before the Lord. I wrote my entire first book about it, so forgive me if I don't indulge in my eating and drinking history here, except to say, good riddance. I no longer worship anything to do with food or drink. Although, you could say, that until I discovered the Eucharist as *the real presence,* I worshiped my abstinence *from* the very substance used on earth in the transformation to his body, therefore, my abstinence became paramount to the spiritual communion. But since I didn't know, I forgive myself for such ignorance.

It's nearing Halloween, when as a child and as an adult, candy was first before everything. Sugar may be called a treat, but it's poison to my spirit, mind and body. Only when I gave up the pursuit of moderation and gave it up entirely, would I hope to never have it again. It required a 12-step program to accomplish, and now it's requiring every ounce of courage to wait until the Eucharist so it has a chance to treat my condition, which is spiritual starvation manifested in the body.

Tonight, however, I feel fed by my own faith in the Eucharist to feed the world.

October 27, 2025

Yesterday I experienced an enlightened moment and have no witnesses: I feel fed by my faith as if I have already received the Eucharist! I looked at the sky as I was walking to church and felt like I was already part of the heavenly banquet. I don't know how else to explain the all-encompassing holiness with no difference between heaven and earth, like I already abide in him.

Then how come when my eldest daughter asked me how church was, I didn't tell her about this? Because I could have said, guess what, *today I became aware that I have been given the gift of faith.* And this is what Satan would love to steal from me. I even had to look it up; yes, faith is a gift in the Bible. Ephesians 2:8-9 says: "For by grace you have been saved through faith; and this is not your own doing, it is the gift of God – not because of works, lest any man should boast."

Faith, defined as a gift from God bestowed on individuals through divine grace. A supernatural gift enabling people to trust and believe in God. That's what happened on the way to church this morning, dear firstborn daughter, if I could share my faith with you. *What's my problem?* Oh, I get it now. Satan has me on mute regarding my daughters.

Then at one intersection a couple of blocks from church, I joined the pace of someone else on his way to Mass. Matthew's been coming to The Holy Name of Jesus since 1966, the year I was born. All my years felt shored up in that intersection of paths. *That many years of Eucharistic expositions have passed before I would be coming for my portion.*

After Mass, I signed up to receive the "traveling vocations cross" the first Sunday in November and take it home to pray with my family for vocations during the week. It travels between parish members' homes during the month of November for a week of prayer at each family's home. I felt this to be an honor and a way to bring a sacred item into my home for my daughters to see and learn about. I also signed up to pray for three months every Wednesday for all Catholic vocations.

October 29, 2025

Riding the bus to Mass, even the bus driver echoes what the priest says to me in the communion line: "God bless you." I'm becoming socially minded, turning Catholic, feeling the seeds of potential campaigns:

"Sell your car, go on foot."

"Give up sugar, flour, wheat, caffeine and overeating."

"Attend daily Mass."

"Pick up a bag of trash of day out in your community."

Often, I have an entire pew to myself at morning Mass, but there's always at least 50 people there on any given morning. Every day there are surprises of all kinds. Today when Father Thomas read Luke 13:22-30, he came to this section: "After the master of the house has arisen and locked the door, then will you stand outside knocking and saying, 'Lord, open the door for us.' He will say to you in reply, "I do not know where you are from'." And right when he said "knocking" there was one loud knock as if on a door. I didn't know the Holy Spirit came with sound effects. He said afterward he knocked the book by accident.

Humor aside, listen carefully and watch. How does the spirit descend like the dewfall? It means quietly and without noticing, as if it occurs in our sleep, but right in front of us, every day, with our eyes wide open, during Mass.

Today is my first Wednesday of praying every Wednesday for vocations. You'll see what it means in this prayer: "Lord Jesus, as once you called the first disciples and made them fishers of men, continue to let resound today your sweet invitation: 'Come and follow me.' Grant to men and women in our day the grace and trust to respond to Your voice."

Is this you? Have you heard *his voice?* I was called to the table. There is a vocation forming, not sure what is beyond writing. As I pray for all vocations, I pray for my own vocation to be further revealed.

I cannot express to you how overwhelming it is to become Catholic. It is not the number of activities. It's my hyper awareness of every little nuance and every single change going on in and around me, about every detail of life and living that I have previously ignored. I need the time to process all of it.

Lord, Mother Mary, Saint Francis de Sales, Holy Spirit, come. Please come in the form of another dream or vision, one of direction. I'm ready for the next divine revelation. I even asked my daughter if I could borrow her pastels, as I have an urge to create the triptych from the dream I had of Mother Mary and the holy water. Something for my three daughters for Christmas? If you knew how much of an artist I'm not, because of how much of a writer I am, you would also wonder what's gotten into me: The Holy Spirit!

October 30, 2025

The revelation came: Nothing like a good old-fashioned cold to put the brakes on. Missing Mass this morning being sick, I instead read from the book Stephanie sent me to prepare to study it with her over Advent. This book by Donald H. Calloway, a convert who leads pilgrimages to Marian Shrines around the world, is a written retreat with wisdom of St. Peter Julian Eymard, who spent his priesthood fostering love for the Holy Eucharist.

I have an entire stack of Matthew Kelly's books thanks to my Catholic friend JoAnne in New Jersey who sent me this library out of her excitement of me being in OCIA. Regularly, she sends me carefully screened Catholic Instagram posts to fuel my journey. And courtesy of one of our OCIA presenters, Mike, I borrowed a book written by my patron saint, Francis de Sales, called *The Catholic Controversy: A Defense of the Faith.* I am only on page 17 of that one, but what is clear is the *kind* way he shares his viewpoints, so they do not come across argumentative. No wonder he is credited with 70,000 Catholics returning to their faith. My Catholic library is burgeoning, and one day I'll add this diary to it!

Though I will continue to transform, the conversion deep in my soul has already occurred. It feels like a restoration to its authentic and original condition. I'm only two months into OCIA classes, and First Communion is still five months away. Perhaps it's because of the changes in the first three months, attending Mass daily, or the fact that Stephanie had me studying the faith since March. I just got the feeling this book is done and has an urgency about it to bring people to the table to get ready for Christ's return.

In addition, the Holy Spirit tapped me on the shoulder again about *Fault Line*, my novel and script in progress since 2010 about "the coming quake." I just renewed my earthquake insurance after fifteen years of not having it. I need to do some groundwork preparation with my neighbors and get my two outdoor sheds ready for two weeks of outdoor living "after the big one hits in the spring." (My thought of being ready is, if you pretend it's happening at a future date, you'll be ready in case it does, because one day, you'll be right).

Plus, now is the time for me to focus on people, and there's something preoccupying about always having my head in the book I'm writing. So, forgive me if it feels like a premature ending. I still write every day so I could conceivably write a sequel to tell the rest of the story.

I have so many plans. Like I already know I want to volunteer on the OCIA team for next year to be one of the Catholic members who helps new initiates during the eight months of classes. I'm even thinking I would devote full-time to the church, placing my financial wellbeing in the hands of the Lord in a non-traditional way. In other words, work full-time for the church, don't just go get a job somewhere. This requires *financial faith.*

I want to learn Latin. I want to learn the Catholic vocabulary more, so that my prayers reflect the kind of wording I hear that I still can't wrap my brain around yet, not even for prayers. Each day I deepen in faith, I acquire more of these skills to interpret my experiences.

There are so many exciting things coming up that I could choose to write about in the diary, such as All Soul's Day this Saturday. We can bring a photo of our departed loved one to share during Mass. Coming up is the visitation of the relic of Saint Jose Luis Sanchez de Rio (put to death because he wouldn't renounce his Catholic faith), then in OCIA we have the Rite of Entrance, our first formal introduction to the church community as a new group on November 9. Advent begins November 30, and Christmas Eve will be with my daughters at our new church.

If you want to learn more, come see for yourself. Catholic churches have the Order of Christian Initiation for Adults, daily Mass, and adoration. Any season is the ideal time to *come to the table* and experience the true presence. Just attend Mass for two weeks, wink wink. Or attend one hour of adoration. This directory makes it easy to find Mass anywhere: www.Masstimes.org

October 31, 2025

When is "the moment" when conversion occurs? We believe it, formally, to be the moment we all take our First Communion in April.

It's exciting that we candidates (baptized already) and catechumens (not baptized yet) get to make our first church appearance on November 9 at the 5:30 p.m. Mass during our Rite of Entrance. Stephanie can't come until the Easter Vigil, so I asked Gloria if she would stand for me in her place and she said yes. Gloria is one who believed my Eucharistic unveiling, where I went one minute from not seeing how, to the next minute comprehending. In fact, she said hearing my story moved her to tears! Oh, to be believed! Most of my life I've been told I'm too intense, esoteric or "out there" for people, when really my experiences are legitimately spiritual. *Here in the Catholic Church, people can't wait to hear who saw what next!*

Meanwhile, it's April 4, 2026, on the Easter Vigil that initiates us all officially into the church at the same time. But I would bet that each of us has our own internal conversion moment – an exciting process to attempt to identify.

I had my moment after last night's OCIA class on Mother Mary and the saints led by our presenter, Mike. There's nothing like becoming Catholic to really help you see just how much potential you *have not tapped.* Our formation director Rich says: "We're all called to holiness."

We covered descriptions of what saints do, and while the list is long, the partial list includes bilocating (being at two places at the same time), levitating, entering into ecstasy, seeing Mary, seeing heaven or hell, raising the dead, curing the sick.

Classmates shared a few jaw-droppers I won't repeat here, but if you join an OCIA class, be sure to tune into other people's stories of encounters with saints and angels, with keen ears.

The moment of the Catholic conversion of my soul occurred for me in the forelight, in a dream. Early this morning, I had a dream where I was still in the OCIA class last night. In the dream, I informed the formation director Rich that *these people in the Catholic faith believe me.* I remember saying aloud to him in the dream, "Seven years this took me!" and Rich responded, "I could see how much it meant to you."

With that line in the dream, Rich was referring to a moment in real class when last night we heard our classmate Isaac share his story of meeting his guardian angel. Mike the presenter in class turned to Isaac and said, "I believe you." That's the moment Rich was responding to in the dream I had, because it struck me as so profound to be *believed,* not just to believe.

Now I know how excited Jesus is that I believe it's really him at the altar, where I've come to the table. And just like I'm waiting for him, he's waiting for me.

People here in the Catholic Church don't just see *you*, they see the *unseen* you, unseen even by yourself. How this dream continuation of last night's class represented my soul's conversion to Catholicism, I don't know. But I did the math on "seven years," and that was the time I had the dream of the transformation by the Holy Spirit in that wedding dress in front of a congregation.

There is much more to come, so won't you join me on the journey to the altar? Volume II of *Come to the Table* is scheduled for publication on April 4, 2026, and I pray the volumes keep coming until my viaticum. What's that, you say? I invite you to look it up. I'll end Volume I now where it began, issuing you the same invitation I received:

Come to the table.

Made in the USA
Coppell, TX
15 February 2026

71376094R20111